GOLD FROM IRON

A HUMBLE BEGINNING, OLYMPIC DREAMS, AND THE POWER IN GETTING BACK UP

GOLD FROM IRON

A HUMBLE BEGINNING, OLYMPIC DREAMS, AND THE POWER IN GETTING BACK UP

**NICK BAUMGARTNER
WITH JEFF SEIDEL**

TRIUMPH
BOOKS

No part of this publication may be reproduced, stored in a retrieval system, or transmitted in any form by any means, electronic, mechanical, photocopying, or otherwise, without the prior written permission of the publisher, Triumph Books LLC, 814 North Franklin Street, Chicago, Illinois 60610.

Library of Congress Cataloging-in-Publication Data available upon request.

This book is available in quantity at special discounts for your group or organization. For further information, contact:

Triumph Books LLC
814 North Franklin Street
Chicago, Illinois 60610
(312) 337-0747
www.triumphbooks.com

Printed in U.S.A.
ISBN: 978-1-63727-545-0
Design by Nord Compo
Photos courtesy of Nick Baumgartner unless otherwise indicated

For Landon, Oakley,
and all the Yoopers—you know who you are

The world ain't all sunshine and rainbows. It's a very mean and nasty place and I don't care how tough you are, it will beat you to your knees and keep you there permanently if you let it. You, me, or nobody is gonna hit as hard as life. But it ain't about how hard you hit. It's about how hard you can get hit and keep moving forward. How much you can take and keep moving forward. That's how winning is done!

—Rocky Balboa

CONTENTS

Part IV

INTRODUCTION

I JUST HOPE MY STORY inspires somebody to dream. The crazier the better. Dreams should be so big they scare the crap out of you.

Or maybe it inspires somebody to do whatever it takes to achieve those goals. Maybe you have to take a job you don't like just to pay for your dreams. OK, so do it. You think I liked pouring concrete? Heck, no. Working concrete beat me up. Hurt my hands. Killed my back. But concrete funded this wild journey and paid the bills. So I'm thankful for concrete. I love concrete!

Or maybe it inspires somebody to get back up…after being knocked down.

Or maybe it teaches somebody a lesson in perseverance. I failed to win anything at my first three Olympics. Got the old wooden spoon. Didn't win gold until I was 40 years old. That's old as dirt for an Olympian. But I refused to quit.

Or maybe it shows how it doesn't matter how old you are, doesn't matter what the youngsters think, doesn't matter how many people doubt you…just keep believing.

Or maybe it inspires somebody to get creative, just to figure out a way to make it happen. I lived out of a van while training for the Olympics, sleeping in back with my dog. But I made it work.

Or maybe it shows the importance of surrounding yourself with the right people. My teammates and my family and my community in Iron River, Michigan, mean the world to me. That's what this story is about. How everybody in my life played a role in getting me to the Olympics.

Or maybe it teaches somebody how to work with others. I won my gold medal, in part, because I was teamed up with Lindsey Jacobellis, the greatest female snowboard cross racer of all time. When you are paired with the right person, when you surround yourself with the right group of people, when you have the same desires and goals, you can achieve something magical.

Or maybe it inspires somebody to get rid of the excuses. It doesn't matter where you come from. It doesn't matter how many obstacles you face. It doesn't matter how many times you get knocked down. Just keep getting up.

Or maybe it inspires somebody to get off the couch and go for a walk, or join a gym, or take up a new hobby, or eat a little healthier, or follow through on those New Year's resolutions. You've got one body; take care of it.

Or maybe it inspires somebody to try something new. That's the only way to find your true passion. I didn't find snowboarding until I was 15—that's crazy old for an Olympian. Most Olympic snowboarders started when they were three or four. So keep trying things until you find what you love.

But more than anything, I hope my story offers a surge of hope. Even when you have failed once or even twice or more, even when things look dire or seem impossible, if you keep working at something, if you give everything in your soul, if you are stubborn and refuse to give up, if you devote your life to something, if you create a life around that goal, anything is possible.

I've got a gold medal in my pocket to prove it.

PART I

CHAPTER 1

ONE SMALL MISTAKE

**February 10, 2022
Zhangjiakou, China
2022 Winter Olympics**

The sun was bright, the air cold and crisp. Long shadows stretched across the snow at the top of the course. I strapped on a black helmet and adjusted my goggles.

My fourth Olympics—maybe my last chance chasing this crazy dream.

"Racers into the gate," the starter announced.

I took a deep breath, nodded my head. My heart was pounding hard. Go time.

"Racers ready!" the starter said.

A TV camera focused on my face, zooming in so close that viewers on USA Network could see a fleck of ice stuck to my mustache. A banner across the bottom of the TV screen read, NICK BAUMGARTNER. OLDEST MEMBER OF U.S. OLYMPIC TEAM, 40 YEARS OLD.

It was so freakin' strange to have your life reduced to one line, because it could have gone in so many different directions. It could have said so many things:

NICK BAUMGARTNER, A BLUE-COLLAR, DOG-LOVING, TRUCK-DRIVING UNION GUY FROM THE UPPER PENINSULA OF MICHIGAN—AND DAMN PROUD TO BE A YOOPER.

Maybe it could have focused on my 17-year struggle to get to this moment:

Nick Baumgartner, the only Olympian who worked construction during the summer to pay for his dream, slinging concrete with a shovel, breaking his back and busting his hands, trying to save up just enough money so he could live out of a beat-up, crusty old van while training.

Maybe it could have focused on my personality:

Nick Baumgartner, a loud and obnoxious guy by his own admission who is actually a fun-loving teenager stuck in a grown man's body, always cracking jokes and laughing, smiling and messing around, trying to keep things light.

Or maybe it could have focused on my strange journey to reach that moment:

Nick Baumgartner, a guy who played college football but gave it up to become a professional snowboarder, failed at three Olympic Games, won X Games, raced trucks professionally, and became a single father known to drive all night just to see his son, Landon.

Or maybe, it could have been even more blunt about my intentions:

Nick Baumgartner just loves to beat the crap out of youngsters half his age while trying to show his son, not to mention everybody else back home in Iron River, that through hard work and persistence, you can achieve anything.

"Attention!" the starter said.

That command signaled the race would start within five seconds. I crouched, my feet strapped to a handmade, custom-built Oxess board, taking several short, quick breaths. One last chance to get ready. The next few minutes would change the trajectory of my life—for better or worse. But I've lived on the edge my entire life, and at some point, you get used to it. You get comfortable in the uncertainty.

I was the most experienced racer in this race—the quarterfinal round of men's snowboard cross at Genting Snow Park in Zhangjiakou, China—and the pressure was insane. I had already failed to medal at three Olympic Games, and I was running out of chances. Every athlete has an expiration date. The moment when the milk turns bad, when your body can't do it anymore, and you get passed by the youngsters—although no one ever really knows when it will happen.

But I was doing my darndest to try to postpone it once again.

I grabbed the handles on both sides of the starting gate, coiled and prepared to explode out of the gate. Snowboard cross is pretty simple to explain—four snowboarders race down the course at the same time. First one to the bottom wins. Simple as that. It's really no different than going to the top of a ski run and racing your friends to the bottom. That's what makes my sport so cool. There are no judges, no scores, no style points. You either win or you lose. Life is black and white in snowboard cross. There is no gray area to complain about.

But it can be crazy dramatic. Snowboard cross is high-speed chaos. We shoot over rollers that look like huge camel humps cemented to the side of a ski mountain. We soar after getting big air on jumps and try to survive a series of wicked turns without falling. The danger is constant.

Over the years, I broke my back and my collarbone, and I crashed more times than I can remember. The metal edges on a snowboard are as sharp as swords. But we had little protection. Football players wear knee pads, hip pads, and shoulder pads, and some even put on rib protection and elbow pads. But snowboard cross racers scream down a mountain, zipping across snow and ice, sometimes banging into each other at highway speeds, sometimes crashing hard to the snow, wearing nothing but a bucket on our heads. A simple helmet.

It helps to be a little crazy. Because snowboard cross is predictably unpredictable—pure chaos, slipping and sliding down a mountain.

The top two finishers in each heat would advance to the semifinals. The other two were toast—thanks for coming, no soup for you. Speed was important but strategy and technique even more so, especially on a slower course like this one.

Crashes were inevitable, like holding a NASCAR event on snow and ice. So broadcasters loved to show the discipline.

———————

The TNT broadcast switched from Beijing to the scene in my parents' living room back home in Iron River, Michigan. Eleven friends and family members crowded together, some sitting shoulder to shoulder on a couch in front of a TV, pumping their fists on cue, clapping and cheering when they saw me. They were in the house where I was raised with my three older brothers, my younger sister, and a bunch of foster children. My parents would take in anybody who needed help, teaching me the true meaning of love and family. Some of the most important people in my life were in that room: Landon; my mom and dad; my sister, her boyfriend, and his kids; and a bunch of Landon's friends from school. None of them were allowed to attend these Olympic Games because of the worldwide COVID-19 pandemic. Foreign spectators were prohibited.

And that sucked.

So my family made the living room look like a colorful TV set, hanging an American flag on the wall next to a red-white-and-blue

Team USA jacket and a handmade posterboard sign that read: Go Nick!

The TNT broadcast switched back to the scene in Beijing. As the camera focused on my face again, the announcers started to re-introduce me to the nation, rehashing how I did at the 2018 Winter Olympics. To the general public, Olympians seem to reappear in four-year intervals, popping into view and then quickly fading into the background.

"His son Landon was at the last Olympics—I met him there," said Todd Harris, the NBC snowboard play-by-play announcer, working his sixth Olympics with the network. "It was really cool in 2018. Nick really wanted to show Landon how hard work pays off, right? Kind of setting goals. No matter the result or winning medals. I remember watching them at the last Olympics. It was a really special moment, even though Baumgartner didn't win a medal."

I finished fourth, which was nothing but no man's land at the Olympics. They give medals for first (gold), second (silver), and third (bronze). But fourth? Nothing. Zippo. It's called the wooden spoon.

Basically, you train your entire life for one moment, getting a chance to compete against the best in the world on a stage so big it can blow your mind; and if you finish with less than a medal, you walk away feeling like a loser, which was always wild to me. Imagine being one of the top four in the world at something—the fourth-best doctor, or the fourth-best singer, or the fourth-best actor, or the fourth-best engineer.

That would be pretty amazing, right?

But finishing fourth at the Olympics makes you feel like a giant failure.

Years ago, ABC showed features on Olympic athletes called "Up Close and Personal." They took you behind the scenes with the athletes and shared their everyday stories. But in 2022, the Games were broadcast on multiple channels—sometimes spread across so many they were hard to find—and the human-interest side of the story was reduced to a few seconds of introduction.

So a moment before the start of my race, TNT put up two pictures of me—"Up Close and Personal" style. They were a silly shot with Landon and another with my dog, Oakley, a black-lab/pit-bull mix rescue dog from the local pound.

I love Landon more than anything in the world. He is my pride and joy—the greatest achievement of my life. Being a dad means more to me than anything, and the only thing I wanted was to make him proud. To teach him how magical things can happen if you make crazy dreams and just go for it.

Oakley was my best friend. We had been together for 13 years. All summer, when I lived out of a van training in Marquette, Michigan, Oakley never left my side. I pulled a mattress into the back of the van between the two wheel wells, and she slept beside me. She went with me everywhere. When I went to a training facility, Oakley was allowed to go in when it wasn't busy. When I went for long mountain bike rides—one of the secret keys to my training—I'd chain her up outside the van, and she waited for me to return. I'd put out water and a big piece of carpet and her memory-foam bed for her, of course.

"Nick has a heart of gold," said Seth Wescott, the snowboard analyst, previewing my race. "In 2011, when he won the X Games, Landon was there as well. I just want to see him pull this one out here today."

Seth and I were teammates for years and I considered him a close friend. I was on the 2010 Olympic Team with Seth when he won his second gold medal. I was so proud of him, and I owed a lot to him. When I first joined the U.S. Snowboard Team, I was definitely an outsider. The team had been together for years, and I didn't know anyone. All the other snowboarders were all good friends, and I was this loud, obnoxious Midwestern kid. A former football player—just another meathead. But Seth was super nice to me. He would tell me stories and give me advice and try to help me. Some of the other guys didn't exactly do that. It was just nice to have someone I could talk to. So we had a long history together—and a heck of a lot of long rides in vans together.

———————

As Seth finished his sentence, the starting gate dropped, and I shot onto the course with the three other racers. I had a slow start, like always. Getting older sucked. Jake Vedder had the fastest reaction and took the early lead, although only by a fraction of a second—less than the time it takes to blink your eyes.

Vedder, a 23-year-old from Pickney, Michigan, was put on this Olympic team at the last second because he replaced Alex Deibold, one of my friends who had suffered a head injury at a qualifying race at the Cortina d'Ampezzo World Cup in Italy.

Julian Lüftner, a 29-year-old police officer from Austria, had the second-fastest start (0.06 seconds behind Vedder). I always gave him crap, telling him that cops are always chasing other people. But if you chase me, you are behind me. He was a really good friend of mine. I was in third place (0.07 seconds behind Vedder). The final racer was Yoshiki Takahara, a 24-year-old from Japan. I've competed against all three of them multiple times.

It was typical for me to start out behind the youngsters. I wasn't surprised. As I've gotten older, my reaction time has slowed, and my fast-twitch muscles stopped twitching so fast and started aching. I've spent the second half of my career having to chase people down after a slow start.

About five seconds into the race, we got our first big surprise when Takahara wiped out going over one of the rollers in the start section. "Down hard is Takahara," Harris said on the broadcast.

He had crashed going over one of those camel humps.

"But it's not over until it's over," Harris said. "Anything can happen even with three remaining on the course."

I pulled into second place, settling in behind Vedder. I was confident I could win a medal if I could just survive the early rounds and get to the finals. I had been riding fast. I just needed a chance to prove it.

This course at the Genting Snow Park suited me perfectly. I felt confident on it after taking third place in the men's big final at the snowboard cross Olympic test event in November 2021. This course was slower and flatter than many courses I had competed on over the years—perfect for me, an aging athlete, somebody who had lost a little strength and explosion. But I could make up for it with knowledge and instincts gained over a lifetime of racing. When you race at a slower speed, it becomes tight racing, and you've got to make split-second decisions—the kind I've made a million times. In a slower race, everything becomes more unpredictable, especially in tight racing. And I was going to need all that wisdom to advance and win a medal.

"Right now, it's the blue bib of Jake Vedder from the United States in the lead," Harris said. "In front of his teammate, Nick Baumgartner. So the Americans, one and two right now. Will they advance to the semifinal?"

We went over a series of jumps.

"Yeah, and I hope they are talking to each other," Wescott said. "They can't back off. They need to work as a team a little bit here to keep Lüftner shut down."

————————

Yes, we actually talk to each other during a race. Even though we are flying down a mountain at highway speeds. Even though we are taking crazy jumps. Even though we are carving hard through turns. Even though we are trying to beat each other. We talk all the time. I've always been super vocal. If I'm going into a corner and there's someone there and they are not leaving me a lot of room, I yell, "On your inside!" I want them to have that information, trying to keep both of us safe. They can do whatever they want with it. I'm 6 feet and 215 pounds. If I yell at you and tell you I'm on your inside, and if you close that door on me, I'm not gonna slow down. I'm gonna f—ing charge right through you. Hopefully I stay on my feet. But I'm not going to give it to you; that's not the kind of competitor I am. If you leave me enough room, there's a chance we're both gonna get through that. If you don't give me enough room, I promise you…if I fall down, you're probably coming with me.

About 42 seconds into the race, I went over a jump and soared into first place as Vedder slipped into third.

"Lüftner hunting them down," Harris said on TNT. "Taking that outside line right there, Seth, can he do it?"

Everything was going fine. We went through turn one, turn two, and a long straightaway that funneled into a set of three big jumps in a row. I made too big of a move off the lip, so I could fly it lower. Jake and I didn't fly far enough and didn't clear the jump. That allowed Lüftner to draft us and get up alongside of us.

Then he slipped in front of Vedder.

"Trying to make the pass," Harris said on TNT. "A little bump-and-grind. Jake Vedder now in third place."

Going into turn four, Julian caught me and cut to the inside.

"Nick is running a great race," Seth said on the TV broadcast. "This is going to come down to one of these photo finishes."

Then everything went horribly wrong. Julian exited into my path and a voice screamed in my head, *Ah! No!*

I was just about to double the next two rollers. I was thinking, *If he keeps coming, I'm gonna get hurt bad.*

I pumped my arms and legs as hard as I could, trying to generate speed on my own. Rather than jumping from one roller to the next, I tried to ride through them. If I didn't, he would exit right into me.

I went to pump the second roller, but I was going too fast, and rather than gaining momentum on the backside, I caught a little air and landed flat, a costly mistake. It was like pumping the brakes on a car while cruising down the freeway. I lost momentum immediately, slowed to a crawl, and the other two shot by me.

"A little mis-timing by Baumgartner," Harris said.

"Oh!" Wescott screamed.

He knew it.

I knew it.

It was over. At that moment, I had almost no chance of winning, much less advancing. Not unless one of them crashed. I had lost too much momentum and too much speed to catch them.

We went into the next corner, and Jake and I kind of ran into each other as he was passing me. But that didn't matter. That wasn't Jake's fault. That didn't affect my race.

I had already lost my speed. I was already dead in the water, and I could already sense my Olympic career coming to an end.

"Jake Vedder now in second place," Harris said. "He's in the transfer position. And right now, it is Nick Baumgartner running out of real estate, circling the drain as we come down. Baumgartner will not make it through."

Circling the drain, all right…my dream was heading for the sewer.

One mistake. One stupid mistake.

I took the last jump standing up, in full submission mode, having already accepted my fate. It was over. The emotion was already hitting me as I crossed the finish line in third place—no man's land in the quarterfinals. Only the top two advanced. I was toast.

"Jake Vedder, who came here to replace Alex Deibold, is the lone American to make it through to the next round," Harris said.

I was crushed. Everything I had dreamed about for 17 years, everything I had worked for, a lifetime of training, a lifetime of dreaming, had vanished in a matter of seconds.

At the bottom, I unstrapped my boots and kicked my board slightly. The finality smacked me in the face—a painful, stinging disappointment. This was my fourth Olympics and maybe my last.

I tried to keep it all inside, like a volcano with a thin, weak cap over the top. But I still had several media obligations. We had to stand by the Olympic backdrop as NBC filmed the results. Vedder was excited. To be expected; he should have been. He was advancing to the semifinals in his first Olympics. But it felt like I was walking through a foggy, painful blur—with all the emotions washing over me.

We walked out and an official grabbed me: "All right, you've got to go to the mixed zone."

The mixed zone was a long, winding plastic fence, set up like a maze, filled with reporters and TV crews on the snow at the base of the mountain.

The first interviews were typically reserved for media members with broadcast rights—like NBC or TNT. Then you continued walking through the maze, like cattle going through a chute, talking to reporters from the wire services. Then a group of reporters from the United States. Then reporters from other countries. You did similar interviews over and over, talking about the race, spending just a little time with each reporter.

I knew what they would ask.

How does it feel? What went wrong? Are you going to retire now?

I couldn't do it. Couldn't answer those questions, not at a moment like this. The pain was too overwhelming and fresh. Besides, I didn't have many answers. I had no idea what the future would hold.

How do you explain everything that went into this moment in a quick sound bite? I had worked construction every summer, pouring concrete—hard, physical labor that left my body beat up—just so I could make enough money to snowboard all winter. I lived out of a van, and I parked it anywhere I could find a spot, because I couldn't afford a hotel while training. I didn't just put my life on hold; I created a life around this one dream, trying to win a gold medal. And—*pfft*—it was gone in a blink. I felt like a failure, like I had let down the entire Upper Peninsula of Michigan. For years, I had received tremendous support from my friends, family, and sponsors—just to get to this spot. To have this opportunity.

Only to waste it.

But there were others…plenty of people who thought I was nuts, who didn't believe in me, and I did nothing to prove them wrong.

Were they right all along?

"I need some more time," I said to a media relations person. "Give me a second."

I dropped my board, sat down in the snow, and cried for at least 20 minutes. I was mad and disappointed and embarrassed. The doubt was creeping in. The reality was screaming through my head: *This is how my Olympics might end? Four Games and no medals? This is where the curtain comes down on a 17-year story? No freakin' way.*

CHAPTER 2

A HEARTBREAKING INTERVIEW

I GOT MYSELF TOGETHER. At least, I thought I did.

Walking to the mixed zone, I took a deep breath, gathered my composure, and headed to the reporters. First up? An interview with NBC.

"Nick, I know this wasn't the outcome you were hoping for," NBC's Hailey Hunter said.

I took one look at her and lost it. It was like the cap broke off that volcano, and all the emotion came gushing out. Disappointment. Surprise. Resignation and the realization that my Olympics career was probably over.

"You worked so hard this offseason," she said, trying to handle the situation delicately. But there was nothing she could say that could have made me feel better. "You had a great run out there, just fell short at the end of the race. What's going through your mind right now?"

My head was screaming, *What the heck am I supposed say? How am I supposed to answer that?*

Normally, reporters had a hard time shutting me up. I loved to talk. But no words came to mind. All I had was emotion. Red-hot lava. I shook my head, still wearing my helmet and racing suit.

"Heartbreak," I said, starting to cry, gasping for air. It felt like my chest was being crushed. Like my world was being crushed. I had spent 17 years of my life getting to this moment, just trying to have a shot, trying to win an Olympic medal, and it was all gone in a blink. One mistake. One huge mistake.

"I don't think people know how much we put into this," I said.

I gritted my teeth, grinding hard, trying not to lose it. I lifted my hand and rubbed my forehead without thinking.

"I put so much time and effort," I said, softly. "And then one little mistake and it's gone."

My mistake. I own that. Nobody's fault but my own. An entire career fizzled out in a split-second.

"I'm 40 years old," I said. "I mean, I'm running out of chances. I got so much support back home and I feel like I let them down. This one stings."

The emotion was pouring out of me. Pure, honest, raw.

My voice quivered. My face contorted. It felt like my heart was ripped out. Right on national TV. And the world was looking inside me.

"It's been really fun to watch you throughout the years," she said. "Do you think we'll see you in the future?"

Oh, gosh, don't ask that, don't—

"What are your thoughts on that right now, or do you need to process it?"

Don't go there.

The frustration and desire and determination welled inside me, hardening me. I was a Yooper. Filled with Yooper grit.

"I ain't stopping on this," I said, defiantly.

All the disappointment and frustration quickly transformed into determination and defiance. Like concrete hardening on a warm summer day. The story of my life.

"I gotta do something better to end it," I said, starting to regain my composure. "Man, I just feel bad. So much effort, and it's just a big letdown. And I mean, I'll keep going. I mean, it's what we do. We fight through the adversity, but…"

I sighed.

"This one stings," I said. "This one stings a lot."

"I know your family's very proud of you," she said, pushing one last button. The only one left. "You saw them cheering you on, on the TV screen there. So great run. Great effort. We hope to see you again."

The interview was nearing the end, but I wanted to send a message back home to the Upper Peninsula, right through that TV camera.

"Thank you, guys," I said. Then I spoke directly to the most important person in my life. My son. "Landon, I love you. I'm sorry, buddy."

The TV broadcast cut away to my family in Iron River, Michigan. It was the hardest interview I had ever given, not to mention the most honest. The video went viral, bouncing across the internet, shared countless times, probably because it was so raw and honest. They would broadcast it again later that night on prime-time TV.

I kept walking through the mixed zone, talking to reporters. I felt like I let down my hometown. I wanted a gold medal not just for myself, but for my family and neighbors and friends and former coaches—all the people who helped me along the way. I wanted to give them some hope and excitement. I wanted to carry a medal around, going to different schools and showing it to kids, trying to give them hope.

I felt like I had let down my sponsors—several helped fund this amazing journey.

I felt like I had let down the Wizard, the guy who made my snowboards. I felt like I had let down my parents and my family. But most of all, I felt like I had let down Landon.

———————

My phone started blowing up.

Some people had the wrong impression: "Oh, your teammate ran into you."

They were blaming Vedder. Thinking the reason that I had lost was because I slowed down because of him.

I immediately told everyone, "Listen, he did absolutely nothing wrong and that was all on me."

My mistake was made well before that moment and, if anything, I feel like I ran into him. It was my bad. The entire race. It was something I would have to live with.

CHAPTER 3

A GLIMMER OF HOPE

ONE OF MY TEAMMATES, Hagen Kearney, came up to me with some surprising news.

"You aren't done," he said.

"What?"

"You get another shot in the team event."

"No, seriously?"

I doubted it. The mixed-team event was making its debut at these Olympic Games, and it was set up like a relay race. They were going to pair a man and a woman on one team. First, the man would race, then the woman. But it wasn't clear to me how many teams the U.S. would get to enter in the event. If we got just one team, I figured they would ask Vedder, because he did better than me in the individual race.

"All right, we better double-check and make sure…but do we *really* get two teams?" I asked. "What's going on?"

"I think we get two teams for sure."

The event was so new I didn't know how many teams we were getting. I thought we were only getting one. When we talked about it in a team meeting, I didn't really pay attention. It wasn't clear to me how my finish in the individual race would affect it.

I had been so focused on the individual event that I hadn't even bothered thinking about the team event.

Later, I talked to my coach, and he cleared it up: "We got four people in, but we don't know who we're gonna team together."

I couldn't believe it.

My coaches laughed at me and said, "How did you not know?"

"I was focusing on other things," I said. "My plan was to just go out there and win."

The more I thought about it, the more it made sense to me.

And I knew just who they should pair me with.

———————

I started getting messages from all over:

"Hey, you didn't let anyone down."

"We are so proud of you."

"You are amazing."

"I know you don't know me, but I just want to tell you, pick your head up, you are good."

The messages came from all over the Midwest. Many from people I didn't even know. I don't even know how they *got* my number. But all the positive messages and uplifting notes helped more than anybody will ever know.

———————

The next day, the coaches told me that they were going to pair me with Lindsey Jacobellis.

I was thrilled but not surprised, because we were the most experienced racers on the team. Lindsey was a superstar, the most dominant female snowboard-cross rider of all time. A 31-time World Cup gold medalist, she had won 10 X Games gold medals and was a six-time world champion. Oh, and she just happened to win the first gold medal of the Beijing 2022 Games for Team USA when she took first in women's snowboard cross. It was like an NBA team getting Michael Jordan at the trading deadline. In his prime. Lindsey was 36, used to incredible pressure and competing in her fifth Olympic Games. We had been friends for years. I had so much respect for her, and they were putting me with her? With the GOAT? I was stoked.

"Hey, everyone," I said in a video that I would post on Instagram. "I wanted to jump on here and let you guys know that my head is not hanging, super proud of what I've accomplished. And I know that yesterday's performance does not define my career."

I shook my head and smiled.

"I also wanted to say that I'm very proud of my interview yesterday, although I could probably use better words than *let down* because I know you guys support me," I said. "And I know you're all proud of me. But I'm proud of that interview because I'm glad you guys got to see the emotions. And you got to see how real this is for us."

I took a quick breath.

"As athletes, we get to do some amazing things. And we get to do that because we're not afraid of failure. We wear our hearts on our sleeves and we go out there every day and we put it all on the line and I hope that inspires some people to get what they want from life."

I punctuated the words with my hands, because I was so passionate and the thoughts were coming from deep within. "And you guys, I appreciate all the messages," I said. "I got so many amazing people behind me, and I really appreciate it all. I love every single one of you guys and I'm ready for redemption in the team race."

I nodded my head. "With Lindsey Jacobellis, tomorrow!"

The video was liked more than 7,000 times, and more than 500 people commented on the post. Some cracked jokes: "You look like Will Ferrell. Congrats!"

Yes, I had been told that once or a thousand times. I considered Will Ferrell to be one damn good-looking dude—especially if you say we looked alike.

The vast majority of comments were encouraging.

"What you said and what you revealed of your inner self after your loss in the men's cross finals was probably one of the most real and honest moments I've ever witnessed in ANY Olympiad I have ever watched!" somebody posted. "Couldn't be more proud or impressed!!"

Then I got one from KC Atanasoff, whose family owns Krist Oil Company, one of my main sponsors.

Nick, I know you're consumed with the Games, so I don't want a reply: In the wake of yesterday's event, I felt it important to write letting you know of how extremely proud we all are of YOU here back home," he texted. "I know that you are experiencing the feelings of understandable disappointment but know that to us, your community and mutually your fans, it is more than an event that makes Nick Baumgartner. You have brought great honor to our small northern town. You have achieved something impossible for most. You have positively impacted many lives through the area and instilled inspiration that has transpired into a sense of community, unity, to all surrounding your accomplishments. Your merits will likely never be forgotten.

We know how dedicated you are. We can only begin to imagine the amount of work you have invested, especially to this year's events in particular. I am so honored to be a small part of this great venture of yours. So give this next one your all buddy. Have fun and embrace it! Above all, win or not, medal or no medal, it's all trivial. You come home the same way you departed, our communities' Olympian that I am proud to call a friend!

I texted him back, "Much love brother. I really appreciate you taking time to message me."

My sister, Ida, sent me a text: "I'm so proud of you and I'll see ya when you get home."

She ended it with three red heart emojis. I wasn't sure if she knew that I had one more race.

"Thanks so much," I replied. "I'm glad I get a shot at redemption before I come home."

I was so excited. I was getting another shot. But to bounce back from this loss, to win the gold, I would have to be strong. I would have to be tough. I would have to be determined.

All the things I learned growing up in Iron River.

PART II

CHAPTER 4

YOOPERS, TROLLS, AND BEAR

Iron River, Michigan

Toughness? I knew exactly where I got that—from my brother Robby. He was my hero—except when he was kicking the crap out of me. Every day, Robby would pin me down and torture me until I begged for mercy: "Okay, okay, I'm done. I'm done."

He'd let go and I'd scream, "Yeah, screw you!" I'd take off running, and it would have been fine. But he was faster than me. Robby would catch me and torture me some more, beat me up again. I could handle the torture and, to be honest, that was why I did it. To get the attention. And I'd take it any way I could get it.

"Okay, okay. I give. I give."

Robby was my oldest brother—six years older than me—and I wanted to do everything just like him. He was a star on the wrestling team at West Iron High School, a star on the football team, and a star on the track team. His work ethic was almost psychotic. He was crazy, putting so much effort and dedication into wanting to be the best athlete possible. One time, he saw a TV show about all these famous athletes taking ballet to work on their balance. So he signed up for ballet, and the closest ballet studio was 45 minutes away. He would finish practice and then have to commute 45 minutes to go to ballet practice.

In the spring, when he went to track practice, I would tag along, and I started working on the hurdles, even though I wasn't on the team because I wasn't old enough. Definitely Robby toughened me up. He set the bar high for the rest of us to follow. And his work ethic seeped into me. Along with a mindset that no matter what, if I wasn't the best athlete on a team, the best player on a team, no one was going to outwork me, not after he set the bar like that.

"What do you think?" my mother asked.

My entire family had gathered for another vote.

"Do you want to take this child in?" she asked.

Then we'd vote. Most of the time, it was unanimous.

Yes, we would take in another child. Yes, we would set another plate at the dinner table.

My parents had four boys and adopted my sister, Ida, when she was two and I was three.

After Ida joined our crazy clan, the people from Social Services asked my parents to start fostering. Obviously, there were never enough people to do that, and my mom was easy—*what, you want me to save the world? Of course. Okay, I'll do it.*

Some of the foster kids stayed for a weekend, if they were waiting to get placed with a different family. But lots of times, we had these kids for two to three years at a time. They were usually from families that were having problems with drug addiction or alcoholism.

All the kids came from our area, and we knew many of them from school.

My mom was raising four crazy meatheads and my sister, Ida, and she did it with so much passion. Everything was about her kids. Even though we didn't have space or money, we always had extra kids in the house, though it wasn't easy financially.

On any given night, I never knew how many extra kids would be in the house, or sleeping on the couch, or pulling up a chair at the dinner table. Whether it was giving somebody a simple ride to the grocery store or offering a bed to sleep on at night, our house was always open to anybody in need. It was like a revolving door, spinning off the most important lessons—to be selfless. To focus on helping others. To sacrifice for the greater good. But mostly to fight like heck, just to get a few minutes in the bathroom.

The most kids we ever had in the house at a single time was eight, and it was hectic as heck. A fight for the shower, a fight for dinner.

Oh man, watch out, here comes Robby. Screw you!

You either walked out of that house tough as heck, capable of holding your ground, with thick skin and a competitiveness embedded deep in your soul, or you didn't survive.

My mom would make the parents of the children come over to our house every couple of weeks so she could save them, too. She was like, *All right, here's the plan to help your kids, so you can get them back.*

Usually, it never worked out that great. But she tried her best.

We lived in a three-bedroom home with one and a half baths. Ida had her own room and my brothers and I doubled up in the other bedrooms with bunkbeds. Tight quarters. My parents ended up making their bedroom in the basement. But there wasn't an egress out of the basement, so they put themselves in danger to keep us safe.

My mom did most of it alone. My dad was on the road four to five days a week, traveling all over Wisconsin and Michigan.

He'd leave Monday at two or three in the morning and come home Thursday night or Friday. He was a pump specialist at a construction and drilling company, and he was on the road constantly, working on municipality water systems throughout the state of Wisconsin. If you had a problem and your town's water pump broke, my dad and his partner would show up with their big truck. They'd fix your water system so that your city had water again. But he would be gone all week. Obviously, he had four boys and we ate a lot of food. Just to be able to pay for the food bill in a week, it was tough. So he sacrificed his home life, living on the road, so we could keep eating.

A strong work ethic was expected. No, it was demanded. When my parents had a cousin or a friend or anyone, really, who needed some help to bale hay, or till a field, or get the rocks out, my parents volunteered us: "Oh, heck yeah, we got kids. We'll send them over."

We went to work, never expecting to get paid. We were just doing what was right, helping our friends and neighbors.

My parents had a few strict rules.

Chores were mandatory.

We had to get a part-time job if we weren't playing a sport.

And if we had free time, we had to go play outside.

Put four meathead wrestlers in a house, add a bunch of adrenaline and testosterone, mix in some nonsense, and something wild was going to happen.

Or break. That was inevitable.

One summer, we smashed out every wall in the whole house. This time, it was to get rid of all the outdated lath (narrow strips of wood) and plaster so we could insulate and drywall. It was funny, because every time my dad would fix something, we ended up putting a hole in it. He'd put up new drywall and my brother Robby would throw a fit and punch holes in it. And I remember they got a double wall door—the hollow doors. Big mistake. That didn't stand a chance.

Wrestling matches, if not drag-out fights, broke out constantly. My mom broke so many broom handles trying to get us to stop because she's about 5'2", a little Italian woman, and we were just beating the crap out of each other. She would get trampled if she tried to jump in the middle of that insanity, so she just started swinging a wooden spoon, a yardstick, whatever. But this one broomstick was the most impressive. After breaking a few broom handles on us, she ended up getting this double-thick wooden janitor's broomstick, and she used that to try to stop us from fighting.

But when Robby and Josh would start fighting, that was a different story. The house was coming down. It was nuts.

My dad stopped fixing holes in the walls. He basically said, "I'll wait until they all move out."

––––––––––––

Once a week, my mom got a night to herself and she would go play volleyball, leaving us to ourselves. Two hours later, the entire house was flipped upside down. As soon as my mom left, we started fighting. Somebody would tick somebody off:

I'm gonna kill you!

For God only knows why. We never had any nice furniture, because somebody would start throwing it around, breaking things, trying to get after each other.

One time, my mom came home from volleyball and found the babysitter duct-taped to a chair. I was probably four or five years old, so I jumped off the roof and started running down the road. But no one ever told the story of how the babysitter ended up taped to a chair.

Another time, my brothers took the boards off the porch and put a rug back over it. Then they ticked off the babysitter, getting her to run after them, so she would fall through the hole in the porch, like some crazy scene from a cartoon.

Another time, Robby got in trouble and threw a dresser down the stairs.

I can't imagine it was easy for my parents to find babysitters, because it had turned into a two-person job. One of our babysitters tried that one time, bringing her boyfriend to keep us in line. When my parents came home, I was chasing him around the yard with a bowling pin.

We were never allowed to have fun toys like snowmobiles, or four wheelers, or anything like that. My dad would say, "Those boys have more guts than brains, so if it has a motor, it's not allowed. They are gonna kill each other. I can't get anything fun like that."

So we always used other peoples' toys.

During the summer, we would drive Joey Linna's four-wheeler around, dragging each other on a plastic sled and putting on life-jackets for protection, and then see who could get whipped into the bushes the fastest. Typical, normal kid stuff.

If you gathered all my brothers in one room, I guarantee you, someone would end up driving, jumping, running over, flipping, or terrorizing everybody else. We were always getting planks and pieces of wood and building some kind of ramp or launching platform to see who could fly farther or higher. Or crash the hardest. To see which one of us could be dumber than the other.

I guess that's how you raise a professional snowboarder.

But I would escape the craziness, at least in the summer, by going over to Joey's house. He was my best friend, and I never had to worry about getting my butt kicked there. He had snowmobiles and four wheelers and his grandma would always spoil us and make us anything we wanted. Having Joey around in the summers was probably the biggest reason I survived my childhood.

We lived in Iron River, Michigan, a town of about 3,000 on the far western edge of the Upper Peninsula. About two hours past the middle of nowhere. We had one McDonald's, one high school, one Subway sandwich shop, and one traffic light. In the *entire* county. At the city limits, a blue sign read, WELCOME TO CITY OF IRON RIVER: WHERE YOU ARE ALWAYS HOME.

It's a place I would never leave for long.

Iron River clings to the Wisconsin border, far closer to Green Bay (141 miles) than Detroit (524 miles). So there were far more fans of the Green Bay Packers, including my father, than the Detroit Lions.

Michigan is basically two chunks of land connected by the Mackinac Bridge—a five-mile suspension piece of engineering wonder.

Some people call Michigan the "Mitten State" because it's shaped like a hand. But that description totally leaves out the Upper Peninsula, the badass piece of land that seems to hover above the hand.

The Upper Peninsula is called the U.P. for short, and anyone from the U.P. is called, quite proudly, a "Yooper."

Anybody from the Mitten, the chunk of land south of the Mackinac Bridge, is called a "Troll" because, as we like to joke, they come from under the bridge.

Yoopers love messin' with the Trolls.

The Upper Peninsula is the size of Denmark, and it's actually bigger than Maryland, but the population is only about 300,000. So, what's in the U.P.? Lots of trees. Amazing lakes. A few towns. A growing number of weed shops (which are legal in Michigan). Pasties (a delicious meat and veggie pie) shops. Kick-ass waterfalls. Deer camps. World-class mountain-biking trails. Scenic turnouts overlooking Lake Michigan. Long stretches of two-lane roads with no houses in sight. Long stretches of jaw-dropping beaches—some with sand, others so rocky you can't go barefoot. Massive mosquitos. Nasty, vicious, biting black flies. Soaring bald eagles. Moose and black bears and packs of wolves. Incredible snowmobile trails. Massive national forests. Mom-and-pop motels. Trucks pulling trailers filled with lumber logs. Oh, so many trucks filled with lumber logs. Snowbanks that tower over your head. (It could snow 200 inches in a single winter.) Fun names like Kitch-iti-kipi. Lighthouses. Pictured Rocks National Lakeshore.

And amazing people. An incredible number of amazing people with an amazing spirit.

Yoopers.

The U.P. is bordered to the north by majestic Lake Superior, the largest body of freshwater in the world. Superior is so big, so deep—and so freakin' cold—that it's like a small, moody ocean. Sometimes, Superior could be calm and serene; other times it grew angry and violent, creating massive waves, destroying hundreds of ships. Like the *Edmund Fitzgerald*, a Great Lakes freighter that sank in 1975, killing 29 men. Gordon Lightfoot immortalized the tragedy in his song "The Wreck of the *Edmund Fitzgerald*."

To the south of the U.P. is Lake Michigan—a far smaller, warmer, more peaceful body of water that stretches to Chicago.

It took a special kind of person to live in the U.P. Cell phone service was sketchy. We didn't have many fancy schools. We didn't have many fancy stores—you had to drive one and a half hours from Iron River to Marquette just to rent a tux for prom. And we didn't have many of the same opportunities as the Trolls. Some people thought that was a disadvantage. But I always said that it was our greatest strength. Living in the U.P. hardened us. It forced us to get more creative, to find solutions. It made us tougher, because we had to fight so hard for what we wanted. We didn't wait for someone to give us opportunities. We made our own, and we fought for 'em.

If nothing else, Yoopers will stick together.

Such good people.

Amazing people.

I always said, "A Yooper will give you the shirt off his back. Even if it's 40 degrees below zero." And it usually is.

———————

One time, Robby brought home an Atari, a video game system, but we could use it only when it was raining or 25 degrees below zero.

So, we spent all day outside, fishing or catching snakes or wrestling or messing with the black bears that would visit us.

Seriously. We used to be visited by a black bear. He'd see us, walk over, and sit behind the house, and we'd be right there watching him. Then we'd walk out the back door, and we'd put all kinds of honey and graham crackers and peanut butter on a stump. He'd just lie down and watch us do it. Then as we went in the house and shut the door, he'd wander over and eat it all. He started coming back all the time. When he wanted more food, he'd stand up on both hind legs and he'd look through the back window at us. As soon as we'd walk into the kitchen and start walking toward the thing, he would step down, walk over, and lie down again. Just 10 feet away.

We got to the point where we thought, *Hey, let's feed the bear outta our hands!*

But we didn't want to get hurt. So we would take the cover of an ice-cream bucket, put stuff on it, and put it through the door, and he would just lick it off. But all that fun ended when the bear went to one of our neighbor's houses and they freaked out. As they were getting ready to head to school, our pet bear was standing up on his hind legs looking through their front door window. So, the DNR had to come and trap him. At least, they tried to. My brother Beau and I messed with the trap so they couldn't get him. We didn't want that bear to get caught.

Free the bear!

Free the bear!

Sadly, eventually they ended up fixing the trap and getting him and moving him.

Another time, my brother Robby climbed into a den with a hibernating bear and took a picture with him. The bear was growling at him, lethargic and out of it. (Kids, never try this at home... we were experts at messing with bears.)

Yeah, I'm not sure why people called us crazy.

One thing drove me crazy. I freakin' hated losing to my brothers. I was obsessed with trying to beat them—at anything. And it probably wasn't healthy. It became an obsession.

My brothers played baseball, basketball, and football, wrestled, and ran track. So, I did, too, following their footsteps, signing up for everything. But it wasn't easy. When I joined a new team or started a new sport, I was terrified that I was going to be bad or that someone was gonna tease me.

I started wrestling when I was in kindergarten and I did it all the way through high school. What an amazing sport. I loved wrestling, not because we were beating each other up—OK, that part wasn't bad—but because of the camaraderie and friendships we built. All these athletes coming together on a team. I got to meet kids from different school districts, and I made so many awesome friends through wrestling.

I also tried baseball by accident. I was too young to be on the team. But I showed up with my mom and my older brother for his practice. My mom went up to the coach and pointed at me. "Excuse me. I know he's too young. But do you think he could play?"

Jim Kralovec, the coach, looked at my shaved head—my mom saved money by giving us haircuts, which meant shaving our heads when she was still learning how to do it.

I wasn't wearing a shirt. I was this little meathead wearing a plastic six-pack holder as a bracelet.

"That kid's playing," Kralovec said.

I loved baseball, was always a big fan of it. But we didn't have a high school baseball team. So, we basically aged out of that sport at 15 years old. We were done. There was no future for baseball for us. But I loved that sport. I don't know whether it was money or funding or the spring weather in the Upper Peninsula—it's hard to play baseball on frozen ground—but I'd have to guess it was money.

I was All-State in football, wrestling, and track.

In football, I was known as a big hitter on defense…and a big hitter as a running back. It never crossed my mind to make a move and cut *away* from a defender or to use my athleticism to *avoid* the defense. I'd just run straight toward anybody who was trying to tackle me. Like my big brother, Robby—just so I could run them over. My class had a great football team. We went undefeated as freshmen and again on the junior varsity team. By my senior season, our varsity finished 6–4 and we got to the playoffs—only the second time in 19 years that we had a winning record—but I didn't get recruited heavily.

So, I didn't have a lot of exposure out there.

I was going to golf my senior year and just have fun with my friends. But Coach Kralovec—the same guy who was my youth baseball coach and assistant varsity football coach—told me, "No, you're not. You're running track because you're gonna win state championships in track and you'll be the only athlete in West Iron County history to become an All-State football player, win a state championship in wrestling, and become a state champion hurdler."

I respected him so much, and I listened to him.

That was exactly what I did. I won all three.

———————————

Years later, after I made the Olympics, I was asked to name a coach who had been the greatest influence on my life, and I picked Kralovec. Because he let me play baseball with the older kids and gave me a chance, I always looked up to him and respected him. He was an amazing coach, and to a young athlete he was super cool. He would lift me up over his head and do triceps dips with me. Throughout my entire sporting career, he always kept his eye on me and watched out for me—like making sure I didn't quit track to play golf my senior year. Not only did I win the state hurdling championship, I also broke the school record in both the 300 intermediate hurdles and the 110 high hurdles. I just respected him so much. Eventually, he took a job as a physical education teacher at Stambaugh, the same elementary school I attended.

Wild how life seems to come full circle.

I just wish more people would volunteer to coach. To help the kids. You don't have to be a great coach. Just be there. Just help out.

———————————

Another thing that bugged me: all three of my brothers were named the best athlete in their graduating class. They all also received an award for being the best defensive football player.

But I didn't win either of those awards, and they never let me forget it.

Everything in our family was a competition. It became an unhealthy obsession.

Actually, it drove me all the way to the Olympics.

Just to be the best in the family—at anything.

Whenever one of us would start dating a girl and bring her home, she would meet my brother Josh and say, "Ooh…he's the *hot* brother!"

Josh was the second oldest. Just an insane athlete—probably the best wrestler out of all of us and probably the best football player, too. His ability on the wrestling mat was unbelievable. So talented. Most of my brothers were meatheads—just big and strong and overpowering, more muscle than brains.

Josh was all about finesse and skill. But Josh did not wrestle in high school. He gave it up and decided to play basketball because he knew girls liked basketball players, and Josh was always the ladies' man.

Ooh…the hot brother.

Josh was just *that* guy that everyone else wanted to be. Just like Rob, he pushed the bar higher for me. He set all kinds of records in football—the single-game rushing record and single-season rushing record. Quite impressive. As we grew up, the same work ethic I saw in my mom and dad and in my brother Robby, I saw in Josh.

But Josh was different in one significant way.

Robby didn't really care about clothing, or his style, or what he looked like, or what he had. He didn't care what anybody said, and nobody was going to tease him about wearing ugly clothes or hand-me downs—because he'd just beat them up.

But Josh was different. Josh wanted the nice stuff. Nice clothes, new clothes. And he had a style and wasn't afraid to work his butt off to get that.

So, I followed him into basketball. I tried, at least. But I wasn't very good. Not like him.

I couldn't score, but I could play defense—that only required effort and toughness. In sixth grade, when they sent me and a couple of friends onto the court, they called it Psycho D. I hustled and banged bodies and ran over anybody in my way, never fearing anybody, trying to get the ball. But I couldn't make that freakin' ball go in the basket.

Clearly, it was shaping the attitude I would take into snowboarding.

Effort and toughness and persistence.

———————

We played every sport they offered in Iron River, so my mom spent most of her time chauffeuring us to practices. We were all wrestlers, so she was at wrestling all the time. Rather than just drive us to wrestling and drop us off, she took over the program and said, *All right, I'm gonna run this.*

She was putting in all kinds of hours running the youth wrestling program, organizing a tournament to raise money for the program, keeping that alive for us.

And she was teaching me an important lesson that I would one day use while trying to find sponsors: You can create your own opportunities. You can find the money, if you want it enough, if you work hard enough, if you are creative enough.

———————

When Ida visited her biological family, I went with her. Just to keep an eye on her. I was afraid she wouldn't come home again. Ida and I were best friends—just inseparable. We were basically the same age. My brothers and I were dirty. We never did our chores. We weren't neat and clean. We were a walking mess. But we could always rely on Ida. She would always keep us out of trouble. She helped us clean up, helped us in the kitchen.

Ida, could you make us some food?

And she would.

My older brothers were like these bigger, stronger guys who'd blow into a room, knock stuff over, destroy everything in sight, and torture you. But Ida was the one person who wasn't going to beat me up. That was Ida. My best friend.

Don't get me wrong; she wasn't always the sweetest girl. There was no way you could grow up in a house with four brothers—especially in *that* house—and not turn into a badass yourself. No doubt, she was a badass athlete. She was a basketball player—probably better than Josh—but she fouled out of a lot of games, because she was so aggressive and tough. Yeah, wonder where she learned that?

She would go down in the middle of the paint and wasn't afraid to elbow a girl, chuck her on the ground, and grab the ball. It was so beautiful. Enough to bring a tear to my eyes.

We were so proud of her for that. My brothers and I protected her, too.

Don't mess with my sister!

———————

I was a mama's boy. Whenever she moved, wherever she went, I was literally wrapped around one leg and Ida was wrapped around the other. She was a stay-at-home mom until we were in school and she took a job with the school system to be close to us. Or maybe it was to keep an eye on us.

She worked in the cafeteria. She would get us up for school and then leave us alone, because she had to be at work on time. That meant Beau and I would get into a fight almost every day. I would tick him off, running my mouth, lipping off, or popping off, because I was the younger brother, and that's what younger brothers did. Obviously, he was just a high school kid who got pissed off all the time, wanting to fight, and he'd beat the crap out of me every day before school.

Countless times, my friends would show up to pick me up for school, and I would sprint out of the house with Beau hot on my tail, trying to catch me. A few times, I dived into the passenger seat and slammed the door, and Beau ripped open the driver's side door and dived across my friend, just to give me a couple more punches.

"Stop it!" Ida screamed.

We never did.

But if I ever needed Beau for anything, he was the first one there to help, no questions asked. Even though he loved to beat me up, he protected me. In elementary school, we had recess on the lower level of the school grounds and the older kids had recess up high on this other spot on the property. One time, I was getting in a fight with the bully in my class, this kid who was just way bigger than everyone. He had a full beard in elementary school—just this monster kid. Here I was, lining up to fight with him. A circle formed around us. Everyone was cheering.

Woo!

Let's go!

Fight, fight, fight!

We were getting ready, and before the fight even started, just out of nowhere, Beau dived over this whole crowd of people who were watching and took this kid off his feet and beat the crap out of him.

So, even though Beau beat me up every day, if I ever needed him, he was the first one to be at my side. He was an absolute animal. Whether he was on the football field, on the wrestling mat, or in the streets getting into a fight, you were going to have your hands full with Beau. I felt bad for the kids who had to wrestle him. He'd come out swinging, smashing his forearms into their faces. Man, it was impressive to watch.

There wasn't a lot of finesse with Beau. He would just stand there, basically saying, *I'm stronger than you, I'm tougher than you, and I'm a little bit crazy—ain't no way you are beating me.*

I suppose that was the attitude I took to snowboard competitions.

Beau was a two-time state champion wrestler. For those keeping score—and we always kept score—I won one state wrestling title, Rob never won one, and Beau got two.

So, Beau won that family competition—and he definitely got in more fights than any of us.

Josh and I were fighters, too—but Beau, any chance he got, he was ready to fight.

I always said that Beau was a little crazy. I'm not even sure he was wired right.

Even though he was beating the crap out of me every day, he was always one of my best friends and he was always there to keep me safe.

Unless he was beating me up.

Toughening me up.

Teaching me how to be fearless.

All the things I would one day need on a mountain in Beijing.

————————

My brother Josh got his first real snowboard in 1989 or '90. Beau and I were younger and we got the plastic ones.

Josh's snowboard was the worst kind you could use and still be allowed to go on Ski Brule—our local ski hill. Our plastic ones weren't allowed. So, I started messing around on a sledding hill behind my house. Learning to take risks. Living on the edge, even as a kid.

But I was a skier before I was a snowboarder.

When I was 10, my parents gave us the ultimatum: either go bowling or go to Ski Brule. For us, it was an easy decision. We went to the ski hill to have fun with our friends and get away from living under rules all the time.

Ski Brule was a pretty awesome place. It was right on the Wisconsin border. Only the Brule River separated it from Wisconsin.

Eventually, I started to use Josh's old board, one with bindings that had three straps. As small as I was, the bindings went up almost to my knees. The thing weighed a million pounds. I would literally have to throw my whole body across the board to get it to turn to get up on edge.

But I was officially one of the cool kids. A snowboarder. At 15.

Even if I didn't know what I was doing.

Nobody did. We were just messing around and figuring it out on our own. Trusting our instincts. Trusting our athleticism.

I tried whatever Josh and Beau did.

Josh and a couple of his buddies pioneered the snowboard scene in our area. He was the first one doing 360-degree jumps, and I was always following him. Doing whatever he did—jumps, tricks. Didn't matter. I wasn't afraid to crash and eat it hard. I would always try.

Josh always had an amazing ability to go bigger off the jumps than anybody else. He was a football player and had football-player power and football-player strength to get up way higher off a jump than anyone else. I always looked up to that, and I tried to copy him.

Years later, people would ask me, "How can you get so high off jumps?"

It was because of the way Josh taught me to ride.

We were always building jumps at Ski Brule, and then we would get caught and the ski patrol would come over and stomp them down, and we'd get kicked off the hill. It wasn't because we were wrecking stuff or being disrespectful or malicious.

Even though I was playing three sports, I always found time to snowboard. Beau and I would go every Wednesday and Friday after wrestling practice or anytime school got cancelled. One time it was 80 below zero with the windchill, and school got canceled, but Beau, me, and all our friends went to Ski Brule.

Yes, it was cold in the Upper Peninsula. You could either complain about it or find something fun to do.

———————

Ski Brule was located near the intersection of Brule Mountain Road and Baumgartner Road. Many assumed that road was named after me, but it wasn't. It was named after one of my ancestors long ago.

My family was one of the founding families of Iron River, and the Baumgartner name was sprinkled across town. On the Iron County Museum grounds, a one-room schoolhouse with a plaque outside the building read, THE PIONEER BAUMGARTNER

School. This one room school was built in 1896. It was moved here in 1988 and furnished by local school systems. Iron County had 80 such schools.

Inside that museum, a display on a wall listed important moments and dates in Iron River history:

1956: Ski Brule Mountain opens to hundreds of downhill skiers. The business boasts being the first to open and the last to close in the U.P. with its state of the art snow-making equipment.

I learned to ski at Ski Brule and got a part-time job there.

1964: The first Bass Festival organized by the Crystal Falls Lions Club is held at Runkle Lake Park. In addition to the fishing, the event has offered canoe races and the iconic "Run Your Bass Off" 5k.

Yes, Yoopers have a fun sense of humor. You've got to be a little nuts to live in the U.P.—a place where the mosquitos are the size of black birds. But I won that canoe race five times.

1968: The first U.P. championship Rodeo is held in Iron River making it the only pro rodeo in Michigan. The event is still going strong drawing thousands of spectators annually.

I never entered a rodeo. Wouldn't mind trying, though. There weren't many things I would not try at least once.

1978: The Sherwood Mine closes making it the official end of iron mining in Iron County. There were 78 mines that produced more than 200,000,000 tons of ore over 98 years.

When the mines shut down, everything changed in Iron River. Stores disappeared, restaurants closed, and people left. The number of kids in the school system shrank drastically. Jobs disappeared and options became seriously limited. It's so sad. The kids in Iron River need some hope. They need inspiration. They need to know that you could make big dreams and achieve them—and every-thing is possible—because we are Yoopers.

1988: The Humongous Fungus is discovered in Crystal Falls. It gained national attention in the 1990s and spawned a popular festival that featured a 100 square foot mushroom pizza. It is the largest organism of its kind, spreading across 185 acres and weighs more than 882,000 pounds.

I was seven years old when they found the fungus. As a kid growing up in Iron River, it was cool to think there was something growing under us, a force linking all of us together, like some magical thing in a movie.

———————

When I was in high school, I started watching X Games on ESPN. They were racing mountain bikes and competing on snow-boards, and it was so cool. Shaun Palmer was just destroying everyone. And I was thinking, *That's what I wanna do. That's where I want to be.*

And I started chasing it.

Professional snowboarding is kind of like professional baseball. You have to start out in the minor leagues. So, that's what I did. I started competing in a grassroots program, a local USASA series, when I was in high school. It gave me an opportunity to start competing and gave me a small taste of the sport. It was super fun just because I loved to compete—in anything.

I competed in USASA for two years and both times I was invited to nationals. It was a chance to see how I stacked up against the best kids in the country, but we just didn't have the money to send me there. I was playing three sports. I didn't have a job other than working at the ski hill on weekends when

I didn't have wrestling meets, and I wasn't making enough to be able to go.

———————————

My brothers kind of paved the way for me.

Or maybe they just wore down my parents.

But I was pretty easy compared to them. I kind of got away with everything. Josh and Beau would go out and party. Rob didn't party at all—but he was still a lot to handle.

By the time it came to me, my parents had seen everything. So if I got into trouble, they were like, *Yeah, whatever. We've seen that before.*

I didn't party much in high school because I was always afraid of getting caught, getting into trouble, and losing sports. That kept me from partying all the time and drinking.

But I still found ways to have fun.

One night, my parents were sitting on the porch drinking beer when the cops pulled up.

"Can we help you?" my dad asked.

"Your son's out on the highway mooning people," the cop replied. "And then he ran into the woods. I'm not dumb enough to chase him through the woods. I'm just gonna wait here."

Apparently, the cops recognized my butt.

Can you imagine that? Having a police lineup…for butts?

———————————

During my freshman year of high school, my English teacher gave us an assignment to pick a career that we wanted to do and write about it. Obviously, I said I wanted to be a professional snowboarder. The next day, she took me out in the hallway.

"I think that's very cool," she said. "That's awesome. But don't you think we should pick something a little more realistic for this career?"

"Absolutely not," I said.

That was probably the first moment that I started fighting for what I wanted.

I did a little sales pitch to her, telling her my reasons why I wanted to become a snowboarder, all the things that were cool about it, and I talked her into it. She allowed me to write the paper.

Don't get me wrong. I love that teacher to death. She remains one of my favorite teachers. She had no bad intentions. She was being realistic, and I was dreaming, like always. I knew what I wanted to do and I knew what I was willing to do to achieve that, even at that age.

After getting to the Olympics, every time I saw that teacher, I teased her about it.

Now, looking back, there was a bigger lesson: someone's always gonna think they know better. Someone's always gonna tell you what you can't do. And you can't buy into that stuff.

A lot of times, when you set outlandish goals, people aren't going to understand you, and they might make fun of you. That's okay. Don't believe those critics.

Just keep going, fight for what you want. Use that as fire. Let it boil in your gut. If someone says you can't do something, you say, "All right, watch me; I'm going to show you."

I had an incredibly late start for a future Olympian—I was 15 years old.

I started on a 400-foot resort that was beautiful in its own way but tiny compared to the mountains my competitors started on.

Most of the kids I would eventually compete against not only started when they were two or three years old, they also started on 10,000- to 12,000-foot mountains. The Swiss Alps. The Austrian

Alps. The Dolomites in Italy. The Rocky Mountains in Colorado. They started in perfect conditions, never learning how to adapt.

But that didn't stop me.

A lot of people ask me, "How did you grow up?" Many of my teammates, and guys that I raced against in this sport, grew up with a lot of money. They're like, "Were you rich?"

I have a simple answer: "Well, not monetarily, but with other things, yes, we were very rich. Rich with lessons of love and support and I think that's vital in our success as we got older for sure."

A few summers before the 2022 Olympics, we had a huge bonfire at my parents' house. All my brothers and some friends were there, and we built this huge ramp. Everybody took a bicycle and we were hitting this jump and using the light of the fire to soar into the air. Everyone was there and we were just trying to wipe out for them. But we made a rule: you had to wear a helmet.

And we never wore helmets when we were kids.

One of my nephews wanted to hit the jump and he wouldn't wear a helmet. We were like, "No, man, you have to have a helmet on."

Maybe that's progress. Maybe that's a sign we're growing up a little bit.

Thinking back on it, maybe my childhood was a little crazy.

But all those fights with my brothers, all the times I got knocked down, all the times I was the smallest kid fighting these monsters—OK, my brothers. All those chips were forming on my shoulder. All of that competition—daily, hourly. All those battles taught me important lessons and set me up for what was to come.

CHAPTER 5

CHASING THE DREAM

IN THE FALL OF 2000, I went to Northern Michigan University to play football as a preferred walk-on. I wasn't given a football scholarship, but I had a chance to earn one. That was all that mattered to me—having the chance to keep playing.

Once again, I was following my brothers. Rob and Josh both went to the University of Wisconsin–Stevens Point—a Division III school about 150 miles from Iron River. Rob wrestled in college and Josh played football.

So, I showed up at Northern Michigan and dreamed of playing in the NFL.

The football was awesome. But it was also eye-opening. Almost every player had been the best player at his high school or the best from his area. Suddenly, I was no longer one of the top dogs. It was humbling and made me work even harder.

There were only two things I could control: my effort and my attitude. As a linebacker, I wasn't even close to being the fastest player on the team. I wasn't the strongest. But when we did sprints after practice, when it could have been easy to loaf or just go through the motions and hurry back to the locker room, I won almost every time. It didn't matter how tired I was. No one was going to beat me. I refused to lose. I guess I could thank my brothers for that mindset.

The school is in Marquette (population 20,629), the largest city in the Upper Peninsula. It's about 90 miles from Iron River, located on Lake Superior. But it felt like a different world. Suddenly, I had freedom. It was the first time I didn't have any rules or parents or supervision. Suddenly, I felt like an adult, and I lived it up. Yeah, I was immature. Yeah, I had a good time. No—I had a great time. Way too much fun. I can't say I studied very much. I made mistakes, learned some lessons, and didn't take school seriously.

I don't think I was college material.

Neither did the dean.

When the football season ended and we finished the semester, I got a letter from the dean letting me know I needed to take a year off and figure out my life. I couldn't exactly disagree.

Uh, yeah, I gotta reevaluate this.

Because what I was doing wasn't working.

I left school, moved home, and got a job at Ski Brule, trying to buy some time to figure out what I wanted to do. But leaving college came with a twist I wasn't expecting. I had been playing sports since I was a kid. My entire life was built around sports— going to competitions and going to practice and hanging out with teammates, one sport blending into the next, one season turning into the next. From football to wrestling to track and then back to football, it was an endless cycle that gave my life structure. I didn't realize that when I left school, I was leaving all of that behind. Suddenly, I didn't have a single organized sport in my life, and it was immediately a giant hole. No more games. No more practices. No more hanging out with teammates.

I missed it tremendously.

———

I was watching X Games on ESPN and thought, *Now, that's what I want to do. I still want to be a professional snowboarder.*

In February 2001, Shaun Palmer, a snowboarder, won an ESPY for Action Sports Performer. Palmer was a superstar, the heart and soul of snowboarding, the World's Greatest Athlete, according to *USA Today*. And he raced everything—boards, skis, snowmobiles, mountain bikes, motorcycles, and race cars.

That's what I want to do. That's the kind of life I want. I don't care if it's snowboard or trucks or whatever.

Palmer was giving me the blueprint, whether I realized it or not. He had won three boardercross Winter X Games gold medals from 1997 to 1999 and was the poster boy for Winter X Games. He was outrageous and tatted up and had his own video game. When I watched X Games, the competitor in me took over, the one who thought I could win every race I ever entered:

I wonder if I can beat that kid if I trained for this? I wonder if I could be that good?

So I decided to try. The plan was so crystal clear in my mind: *I'm gonna get a job. Make some money. Save it up. Move out West. And start chasing that dream. I'm gonna be a professional snowboarder, just like I told my teacher my freshman year of high school.*

Then, I got lucky. An opportunity just popped up out of nowhere. Al Highline, my old babysitter's husband, called my parents' house and asked, "Do you have any boys who can work? I can get him a job making $21 an hour."

It was a lot more than I had made at Ski Brule or the $9 an hour I was making building pole barns and garages.

"Hell yeah," I said. "Sign me up."

It was perfect. I started that job in August 2001, the summer after I left college.

Obviously, when I first started, I wasn't worth $21 an hour, but I was working hard, learning, and saving a lot of money.

Bob Jurasin, one of the Northern Michigan coaches, met with me and offered me a last-second chance to return to college: "Come back and you'll play football for four more years."

"No, I'm trying to become a professional snowboarder," I said.

Crazy? Sure. I had been in different snowboard competitions since high school, and I was winning and getting on podiums, but I was stuck in the minor leagues of snowboarding. Actually, I was probably below that. I was not racing against the big dogs. I wasn't even racing in snowboard cross, just competing in freestyle events. I didn't even know what to do. There were no professional snowboarders who lived near me. No one I could ask for help. No one who could give me advice. No one to teach me the little tricks of the sport. No one I could even try to copy. I didn't know what I didn't know. But I had these nagging questions burning inside me: *Could I beat somebody great like Palmer? What does he have that I don't? How do you even get there? Could I hang with the best of the best?*

I was certain I could do it. But I knew I had to leave Iron River. I had to take the biggest jump of my life.

March 2002
Mammoth Mountain, California
USASA National Championships

It was my first nationals. The first time I ever left the Midwest. The first time I ever saw a real mountain. And the first real boarder-cross event that I ever entered.

I didn't really have any technique. When I was racing in the Upper Peninsula, a couple of us would just sit on the snow and when the starter would yell "Go!" we would rock up onto our boards and jump forward to gain momentum. Then, we would race through the park. Because of my competitiveness, I would usually overshoot all the jumps and beat the heck out of my knees just to make sure I won by quite a bit. But that was nothing.

I was suddenly in the big time. This competition was massive—there were 21 different age groups, including an adaptive division for amputee snowboarders. They called it the "largest snowboard competition in the world," with more than 950 competitors. Their ages ranged from five to 60.

I got there and freaked out. On the chairlift going up the mountain, after getting my first real view of the place, I was scared. Thoughts raced through my mind: *Oh my god, this is real...and we're going over Mammoth Snowboard Park.... Dang, look at that...look at that run....this is huge...so freakin' big.... What have I gotten myself into?*

It was a terrifying but familiar feeling—the same emotion I would get every time I joined a new sport when I was young. I was scared to death inside, so nervous that I was trembling. It was almost debilitating. I got to the top and I decided that I needed to hit a jump to get the nerves out. I needed to figure it out. And I tried to talk myself into it.

You got this. This isn't bigger than you. Come on man, hit this jump. Do it now! You can do it. Don't chicken out. Get going.

If I kept thinking about it, kept freakin' out, I was gonna psych myself out. So, I did it. I went as big as I could off the first jump, which happened to be the biggest jump in the park. I hit it without looking at it. Without seeing how big it was. Without realizing the ramifications. Without checking the landing area. Without any thought or preparation.

But I took that jump with conviction. I jumped like my brother had taught me, using all those football muscles, all that football-player strength, just like I had done for years in Iron River. The big problem that I realized in the air?

Oh, no!

The jump went left to right, and I jumped off it right to left. I landed in the flats, crashing violently, knocked myself out, and shit my pants. Seriously. I shit my pants on my first run at my first nationals and flat-out knocked myself out. When I woke up and opened my eyes and looked around my friends were like, "What the hell were you thinking? Wow, you're an idiot."

I couldn't argue. I was an idiot. But I was at nationals, and I knew this was what I wanted to do.

Technically, I didn't qualify for boardercross at nationals because we didn't really have that discipline in our series. When I was signing up for the other events, I qualified for giant slalom, slalom, slopestyle, and halfpipe. So, I approached Tom Collins, the organizer.

"Can I sign up for boardercross?" I asked.

"Did you qualify?" Collins asked.

"We didn't really have this event," I said. "So, no one did."

"OK," he said. "Absolutely."

In that moment, a career was born.

In the first heat, I was a little timid. When the gate dropped, I came out last and had to pass everyone in order to win and advance.

In the second heat, I started to figure it out. I held the lead from start to finish.

In the semifinals, I learned a quick, important lesson. I was leading going into the first turn and the guy behind me made a mistake, cut the corner, and T-boned me, sending me flying off the course.

I was super bummed, assuming my day was over. I was talking to people at the bottom, just hanging out, until someone told me that I needed to get to the top because I still had to race again.

A small final? What the heck is that?

I had no idea that there was a big final, where they were competing for first place, and a small final—kind of like a consolation prize for the next group of snowboarders.

I got my butt up there and won the small final, and I was hooked. Everything seemed so clear.

"This is what I'm going to do," I told everyone. "I'm gonna make this my job."

Just like I had told my teacher. It was happening. It was like a light had come on and that dream was glowing inside me.

It's time. I'm gonna take my shot.

In fall 2003, my plan was to move to Colorado. I had worked all summer and saved up a bunch of money, and I had a loose plan—just get to Colorado and figure it out. I had met a group of kids from Colorado at nationals (Gregg and Justin Stem), and we stayed in touch. I hung out with them again in 2003 in Maine and we became good friends. They offered me a room to rent at their mom's house in Durango, Colorado.

"Sounds cool. OK, sure. Let's do it!"

But two weeks before I was about to leave, I found out I was going to be a dad.

We weren't really dating. Tina Sundelius and I had broken up and then gotten back together. We were in that awkward, on-again, off-again stage—right around the time we were realizing it was over for good.

But one night we hung out. Messed around. Next thing you know, we're gonna have a kid. I was stunned and afraid and figured my dream was over.

New plan: I would stay in Iron River and get a real job and help raise the baby.

Then, Tina did the most amazing thing.

"Keep going for it," she said. "If you don't, you'll regret it. No way I am taking the blame for that. We'll figure it out."

So, I had several months to keep racing before the baby would arrive.

The first race was an X Games qualifier in Truckee, California. The big problem? I didn't have enough money. But when I was home for Christmas, I received an incredibly generous offer from Chris Hughes. He was the father of one of my classmates and football teammates who had died tragically in a car accident. Hughes owned a towing company in Iron River and offered to sponsor my trip to California. He just gave me a check for $900.

"Thank you!" I said, although the words seemed hollow compared to what I was feeling.

How could I possibly thank somebody enough for giving me a shot like this? For being so generous? For showing so much faith and belief in me? For reaching out and helping me when I needed it so badly?

The generosity of Yoopers—specifically, the generosity of people in Iron River—was amazing. So, I drove halfway across the country to stay with my godmother's old boyfriend. But the race didn't go well. I was taken out by a rider in the first heat and had to drive back to Colorado with my tail tucked between my legs. My X Games invite went up in smoke, and I'd have to wait another season to try to get it.

The second race was held in Crested Butte, Colorado, in the Rocky Mountains. But there was a nasty snowstorm, and there was no way I was going to be able to drive my little Mitsubishi Eclipse through the mountain pass to get to the USASA Southwest event.

I called Tom Collins, the organizer, again.

"Don't worry," he said "You can still qualify if you just win a big event, the US Extremes boardercross. If you win that, you'll qualify."

So, I drove over to Crested Butte from Durango, Colorado. When I got there, I saw all these people rubbing crap on their boards. And I was thinking, *Oh God, I don't know what I'm doing here. I don't even know what they are doing.*

There was this Swix guy peddling little envelopes of race paste.

"Hey, what do you got there?" I asked. "Can I put some of that on my board?"

Briefly, Mr. Swix Guy showed me how to do it and let me handle it myself. I did it and got in the first heat with Nathan Park, who had taken second at the event before, and this other guy, Ox Malloy, who won it the year before. Nathan's brother Jonathan was the fastest qualifier.

Everyone told me, "Dude, you are going to get your butt kicked."

I was like, *All right, here we go. I finally get a chance to see how I stack up against these guys.*

Then I freakin' beat them.

Mr. Swix Guy grabbed me and told me firmly, "You aren't touching your board anymore."

So, he started waxing my board and I ended up winning the event. My first televised boardercross event. The first time I won prize money—$1,500. It was awesome just to go there. Just to win.

Because I needed it so badly.

———————

March 2004
Angel Fire, New Mexico
USA Snowboarding Association
Championships

The USASA championships were a mess. A week of unseasonably warm temperatures turned the snow into slush, and streams of water were coming off the mountain. Two feet of the resort's snowpack melted over a 10-day period and most of the mountain was bare. Even though the temperature was in the 70s, there was enough snow left for more than 1,200 amateur competitors in 32 age groups. I mean, there was a 5-year-old and a 70-year-old. Back then, California-based USASA organized 450 snowboard and freestyle skiing events around the country at 200 resorts for more than 4,000 competitors.

The boardercross was a half-mile downhill race with six competitors racing side-by-side per heat. It was still the minor leagues of snowboarding—we weren't going up against the top professionals. But luckily, I was entered in the snowboard cross open class, and if you won at that level, you got an invite to the X Games. That was enough for me. The organizers said that event was bringing together "future Olympians," and they couldn't have been more right. One of them was Alex Deibold. Alex would become an Olympian and turn into somebody I'd compete against for nearly 20 years, growing into a friend and, eventually, my roommate.

At Angel Fire, I had no extra money, and I was sleeping in my car in the parking lot. My car had a flat tire, so I couldn't go anywhere, but I'd just start the car and turn on the air to try to dry out my soaking wet boots.

After a couple days, it got nasty. That car smelled like someone had died in it.

When the mother of one of my friends, Chris Sleeman, found out that I was sleeping in my car, she insisted that I come sleep on the couch in their condo.

Thank you. Thank you. How can I ever thank you?

The event was huge. It was the biggest winter competitive event ever held in New Mexico, according to the organizers, and more than 1,000 spectators showed up to watch—probably because it was so warm.

I won the event and got my first invitation to X Games, which was like winning a minor league baseball game and getting called up to the major leagues.

Everything was coming together. I could feel the opportunity right there, just waiting to be grabbed. But snowboarding would have to wait. Because I was about to become a dad.

July 9, 2004
Iron River, Michigan
Dickinson County Hospital

"Is there anything I can do to help?" I asked.

Tina was in labor, and Landon was breach.

They had given her an epidural, and it had started to wear off a little bit.

"What can I do?" I asked.

"Yeah, you could pull on her hip one way and push on her lower back the other way, twisting her body a little bit."

I did that every time she was having a contraction because she was in a lot of pain.

After about 45 minutes of pushing and pulling on her through each contraction, my muscles became fatigued, and I started shaking. Yeah, I know. Sounds bad. I'm not complaining. She was doing the real work. She was the one experiencing real pain. But I quickly learned a big lesson: don't shake a woman in labor.

Landon was stuck, and the doctors couldn't get him out. They had to do an emergency C-section. I was allowed in the room as they were doing it. It was crazy. They were so precise with a scalpel, cuttin' her open, and then they so precisely cut the next layer, and then they took a cauterizing knife and they cut the next layer, and then the scalpel again. Then the cauterizing knife again and everything was super precise. Then—this part stunned me—they just put both hands inside her and ripped her open like a deer.

I thought, *Are you freakin' kidding me? You go through all that, so precise and so nice, just to finish like that?*

Landon came out and I cried. It was funny; he had kind of a conehead because he'd been stuck in there, and I had to laugh because he looked like my dad. The same bald hairline and the same shape. But it was love at first sight. When I saw Landon, my heart melted. Didn't matter how much of a derelict I was, or how immature I was. Look what I did—no, look what *we* did. But it was also terrifying. I had no idea how to be a dad. I wasn't qualified for this job.

I was 22 years old.

Tina was in the hospital for five days, so I stayed on a cot in the hospital room. I wanted to learn how to crochet—a popular thing in the snowboard world, so you could make your own hats—and I wanted to make Landon his first hat. So, I was in there, spending five days in the hospital with him, learning how to crochet. Landon's mom and I were both scared. We knew it was not the perfect way to do things. And we had no idea how to do this.

———————

January 2005

Okay, it's time. I gotta go do it.

I had started to taste a little success. But I still didn't know how I stacked up against the big dogs. So, I decided to go for it. I didn't have much of a plan, but I went online and I found some races where I could face the best of the best. I printed off MapQuest directions, jumped in my little Mitsubishi Eclipse, and drove 39 hours to Oregon for a huge competition. I had no place to stay, no plan. But I needed to get there. I was gonna sleep in the parking lot in my car if I had to.

Then, my aunt Regina, who lived in Portland and owned a nursery with her husband, caught wind of what I was doing.

"You are taking that car?" she asked.

"Yeah," I said.

"No, no, no," she said. "Let's switch cars. You can take my 4Runner."

Then she said, "Where are you staying?"

"I'm gonna go up there and crash on someone's couch," I said.

"You don't have a place to stay?" she asked. "That's not happening."

She called up and got me a room and gave me a car, so I could go up there and give it a try.

Thank you, I just can't thank you enough.

When I got there, I was in awe.

Look, the U.S. Snowboard Team. All of them are here. This is so sick. I get to race against these guys.

I was still trying to figure it out, still new to the sport, so I was kind of reckless—to say the least. After some training and qualifying runs, I overheard the head coach, Peter Foley, telling his guys, "Stay away from that kid. He's reckless."

Well, thanks, buddy. Get used to it.

He wasn't wrong. I was reckless. Early in my career, I was super aggressive. I had one thought going down the course: *Gotta win. Press harder. Go for it.*

I didn't know what I was doing. Didn't know how to prepare my board. Didn't even know how to turn. If a course had turns—and all of them did—I was in trouble. I'd scream down the course, straight-lining it, crashing all over the place, getting up—and keep going again. Refusing to stop. Just a wild child going down the hill, the kid who used to get punched by his brothers and wasn't afraid of anything or anyone. I was fearless. I was super aggressive and wanted to go fast but had no formal training on proper technique or strategy. My dad always said his kids had more guts than brains, and that's what I was like on a snowboard.

I was not afraid to go as fast as possible. If there was a corner or a technical jump that I had no business taking because I didn't have the skill to handle it, I did it anyway. And I crashed all over the place. Whatever, get your butt up, keep racing, and chase them down.

Even though it was my first time facing the stars from the U.S. Snowboard Team, even though Foley said I was reckless, even though I was basically taking a football mindset into a snowboard competition, I took 10th place at that event, and it got me noticed.

I think I showed them something. My fearlessness. My desire. My competitiveness. I was going to fight and never back down. That's a trait you can't really teach, but if you find someone who has it, you sure can teach them the rest. And I was aching to be taught.

———————————

January 2005
Aspen, Colorado
9th Annual Winter X Games

My mom, my dad, my sister, and I drove from Iron River to Aspen for my first X Games, and we had no idea what we were getting into.

Holy crap...here we go.... Those jumps are huge...everything is huge.... Is this gonna be one of those moments like I had in Mammoth, California?

Obviously, I had improved since Mammoth. A little. But still, it was terrifying.

OK, I've got to figure this out. Work your way through it and see what happens.

Winter X Games had a little bit of everything—skiing, snow-boarding, snocross (snowmobiles racing on an oval track lined with rollers and jumps), and freestyle motocross (aerial stunts on jumps of 45 to 90 feet). It felt like I was like getting dropped into the big time. There was nearly $300,000 offered in prize money in snowboarding alone, and it was surreal. Just to be there. I had grown up watching X Games, and now I got to compete at them?

How sick.

A crowd of close to 50,000 was expected to attend the event, and for the first time, ESPN was airing it live. There were huge stars like Shaun White; the old Flying Tomato was racking up seven figures. And there were people like me—nobody even knew who I was.

The top snowboarders in the country were coming off the world championships in Whistler, Canada. Seth Wescott had won the gold—of course, he had. Lindsey Jacobellis had won the women's event. And the freakin' *New York Times* did a preview story on X Games, perhaps summing up what the country thought of the event, calling it "a kind of subversive Olympics," "a celebration of daredeviliry," and a franchise that was a "worldwide sporting subculture that focuses on high-risk, envelope-pushing competitions."

Hmm. OK. I was guilty of "sporting subculture" and "envelope pushing," so maybe I was in the right place after all. But the *New York Times* also mentioned how X Games was changing: "Once derided as a tribe of pot-smoking slackers, many of the athletes here are now of the world-class, year-round-training variety, men and women who compete on professional circuits around the world and are supported by commercial sponsors."

I was a former college football player, so I guess I was part of the new wave of athletes, and I ended up taking ninth place. Which was thrilling.

Going up against the absolute best, facing racers who had just competed at Worlds, and I finished in the top 10? Man, it was sick. It was good enough to get an invite back for the next season, and that was huge for me. I felt a touch of validation and a strong sense of conviction:

This is gonna happen. No doubt in my mind. I'm on my way.

But I was also learning about the unpredictable, dangerous side of this sport. Ben Jacobellis, Lindsey's brother, crashed in the prelims—after Nate Holland clipped the back of his board—and Ben was carted off the slope on an orange sled.

Predictably, the big names wound up on the podium. Lindsey, who was just 19 years old, won her third straight X Games, and Seth Wescott finished second.

But I wasn't done.

I was invited to compete in a relay race, a really weird event in which they paired a male snowboarder with a male skier. They called it "ultracross," and they put names in a hat, basically, to select who would be put together. One guy went up and picked out the name of his partner.

The Crist brothers—Reggie, 36, and Zach, 32—from Sun Valley, Idaho, went up to select. They were legendary skiers and former members of the U.S. Ski Team—just big-time names. I mean, Reggie had competed in the downhill at the 1992 Olympics.

So, Zach picked a name and said, "Baumgartner?"

I knew what he was thinking: "Who the heck is Nick Baumgartner?"

So that was how we ended up teammates in my first relay race at my first ever X Games.

It was funny; he made a mistake in the first round, and I had to pass everybody to be able to qualify through to the next round. So, I saved his butt. Then, in the second round, he rode well and I made a mistake. In the small finals, we did all right and finished in eighth place.

What an unforgettable experience. To compete at the freakin' X Games and to finish in the top 10 in both events.

My snowboarding was taking off.

But I was having serious money problems.

The company that I was working for decided to close up, and I was out of a job. In the spring, I felt like the biggest piece of crap. Tina's mom had to buy our groceries and she let me have it for not pulling my weight. I felt like a complete failure, and she was right. I needed to be able to provide for my son and his mother. It was my responsibility. And I was failing.

The next summer, I started a new job working with concrete at a construction company out of Green Bay. Just like with any first job, I was definitely scared. I wanted to make sure that everyone liked me. So, I worked as hard as I could.

The orders were simple: *Shovel! Rake!*

I could do that. I wasn't the best, but I had three years of experience, and I was a hard worker.

On my third day on the job, I got a call from U.S. Snowboard with a surprising invitation: "Hey, we want to invite you to our snowboard camp in Mammoth, California, the first week of June."

That was just two weeks away.

"What?" I asked. "Huh?"

I was stunned. I went into the office at work. "Hey, I got a problem," I said.

They were probably looking at me and thinking: *Man, what the heck; this kid just started, and he's already got problem?*

I told them the story. "I have a shot to fight for a spot on the U.S. Snowboard Team and I got a shot at the Olympics."

They were like, "Well, what's the problem?"

"I just started working for you guys," I said. "And I got no money."

"What can we do?" they asked.

"I need to miss a week of work," I said.

"We will take care of you," they said. "We'll give you a week and a half off of work. And we'll give you $1,200 to go."

I was stunned.

"We're going to take $100 out of your paycheck for the rest of the summer," they said. "Does that work for you?"

"Damn straight it does," I replied.

I went to the training camp, and they paid for my trip. I worked there for the rest of the summer. It was huge—they were helping me chase my dream, even though it still wasn't easy, being in one state and my son being in another. In Green Bay, I was crashing at people's houses because I had just started and I didn't have money for hotel rooms.

We worked for a lot of municipalities and did a lot of concrete sidewalks; curbs and gutters around the city; a Walgreens. Work like that.

I didn't really have a shot at the 2006 Olympics because I didn't meet the criteria to be able to go to the qualifiers. I didn't have enough points built up. My goal was more long-term, looking ahead to 2010.

Landon was almost a year old, and he was staying with his mom. We had gotten back together to try to do the right thing and be there together for him. I was in Green Bay and would drive home as often as I could. Usually, about three days a week, after work, I'd drive two hours, spend time with him, and then drive back to Green Bay at three in the morning. There was no way I was going to miss him taking his first steps.

In 2005–06, I was asked to join the U.S. Snowboard Team.

I was on the C team. The A team got funding, but members of the C team were provided things like uniforms and coaching. When traveling, we could ride with the A team in their vans. Basically just hitching a ride.

It was amazing just being on the team. But I was still super aggressive. I had trouble with little things—like turning. OK, that's a big thing. So, I crashed constantly. I didn't know how to prepare my equipment, didn't know how to turn, and didn't know how to memorize a course.

At my first World Cup, after a bunch of training on the course, I still didn't know it. Or how to remember it. So, I went into the first run, and I was just hyper as hell.

Gotta win. Go hard. Go fast. Go big.

I was going through the jump section, and I knew there was a big step-up on the course. I was going to have to pop it really hard. When I came to it, I popped as hard as I could—only I did it on the wrong jump, a smaller jump, the one before the step-up. I landed in the flats and wiped out.

I totally messed up; totally forgot the course.

By the time the second round was supposed to start, it was snowing so hard that there was no chance of my qualifying in the second run. I was done. Just because I didn't know how to memorize a course. Just because I was full-peg, full-throttle, all the time. I never took time to slow down and figure some things out. And my aggression was biting me in the butt.

———————

Still, I thought I had it all figured out.

I went back to pouring concrete, and I had a plan. *I'm gonna work all summer, pouring concrete. Work my butt off. Make a lot of money. Then, when it gets cold out, and we can't do it anymore because the climate is too harsh, I'll get laid off and take unemployment every two weeks, just so I can keep snowboarding. I'll go back to the U.S. Snowboard Team and keep doing the thing I love to do most, shred and have fun.*

But everything was about to change.

CHAPTER 6

LOSING MY SPOT ON THE TEAM

I'M IN THE BIG TIME. *This is where I'll always be. This is my life now. This dream is happening.*

As a member of the U.S. Snowboard Team during the 2005–06 season, I felt like I had made it. Even though I wasn't fully funded, I was on the C team, which allowed me to receive a uniform and coaching and to hitch rides to events.

The guys on the A team were fully funded. But that didn't matter to me. Not yet. I figured that was only a matter of time until I climbed some more. I was on my way. That was just the next step. It was all so inevitable.

Even though I didn't really know how to turn and I had a hard time memorizing the courses.

But, look, I made it!

Maybe I got lazy.

Maybe it was just too much for me. Maybe I got satisfied and content. Maybe the success made me let up a little. Michigan State basketball coach Tom Izzo, a fellow Yooper, always called it "getting fat and lazy."

And I was guilty as charged. I wasn't working hard enough to improve. I wasn't learning the little things.

I got cut from the team. Flat-out cut. I wasn't asked to return to the U.S. Snowboard Team for the next season. It was a huge setback. A painful slap in the face.

It was completely embarrassing, the first time that I had ever gotten cut from a team in my life.

What's everyone gonna think? How is this gonna look to all those people who have supported me? To all those people who believed in me? How's this gonna work out?

I didn't meet the criteria. But Peter Foley, the U.S. Snowboard Team coach, didn't tell me what I needed to do to get back on the team. Basically, he left me there to figure it out on my own. It's hard to get much confidence when the coach doesn't communicate with you.

That wasn't his coaching style, especially at that point in his career. Members of the official team were all the cool guys, doing the snowboard thing, and I was the outside jock—the football player—on the outside looking in. Nose pressed against the window. Unable to get into the secret club.

Admittedly, I might have rubbed people the wrong way. I was a loud character, probably a little obnoxious to some.

And I got cut.

It was more than embarrassing; it was a massive hit to my ego and confidence. It felt like they had slammed a door in my face. Without being an official member of the team, I was not eligible to get any funding. No more uniforms. No more bumming rides. No more coaching. And because I didn't get the results the year before, no World Cup races that season.

I felt stuck. Like my dream was evaporating before it ever really took off.

I couldn't do it on my own. My family wasn't rich. We didn't have a secret stash hidden away. I didn't come from money. I came from the Upper Peninsula of Michigan. I had a son and bills and I was backed into a corner. I had to do some soul searching: *What went wrong? Whose fault was this?*

I came to a simple conclusion: there was nobody to blame but myself.

I was the one who didn't know how to turn. I was the one who had a hard time memorizing the courses. I was the one who wasn't prepared. I was the one who didn't know the techniques. I was the one who didn't know about the equipment. Obviously, it would have been nice for the coaches to help teach me, to show me what I was doing wrong and how I could improve, but they didn't do that. And ultimately, it was on me to do my homework and figure it out.

I wasn't as dedicated as I should have been. I didn't focus on all the small details that mattered the most. And it was a serious kick in the butt.

The most important thing to me—other than my son, Landon—had been ripped away, and I vowed to never let it happen again: *There's no way I'm giving this up. There's no way I won't fight for this.*

So easy to say.

So much harder to do.

First, I had to find a way to make it work financially. In the offseason, I worked construction, pouring concrete, trying to save money. But the bills kept mounting. Having a kid was seriously expensive.

My brother Josh owned a construction company in Charleston, South Carolina, and he was doing pretty good. Josh worked in commercial construction, going into buildings and putting in drywall and drop ceilings.

So, Beau and I went down there and worked for Josh.

Josh was a machine. He had an amazing ability to make relationships, deal with problems, and always keep his cool. He was the only one of my brothers who was so organized and clean. The rest of us were slobs. We would just leave stuff laying everywhere, never organized, always losing stuff. But Josh was different. Josh liked his stuff organized.

I watched him, studied him, and something was starting to become obvious to me:

That's how I have to approach snowboarding. I have to be more like Josh. Just working my butt off isn't enough. It's more than that. I have to be organized. That's the only way to be successful. That's the only way to take advantage of opportunities. I have to be prepared for them. I have to have all my stuff in order. I have to be smarter. I have to look at problems clearly and search for solutions. What's my biggest problem? I can't friggin' turn. I have to learn how to improve my technique. I can't do this halfhearted. I have to build my career, brick by brick.

I went into desperation mode.

Working construction wasn't enough to fund this dream. Donations from family and friends weren't going to be enough.

Think like Josh. Identify the problem. See it clearly. And search for solutions.

I needed more money, and I wasn't above begging.

I got out the phone book, went through the Yellow Pages, and found every business on my side of the county. I sent each of them a letter, describing what I was trying to do:

I'm fighting to become a member of the U.S. Ski and Snowboard Team. I'm trying to get to the Olympics. I want to bring a medal back to the Upper Peninsula. I want to be an inspiration to all the young kids in our area. But I can't do this alone. I'm trying to raise money to keep my dream alive. If you could provide some financial assistance, any amount, it would be greatly appreciated.

Some businesses gave me 50 bucks. A couple donated $500.

I raised a couple thousand. To many, I'm sure, that didn't sound like a lot of money. But it was like pumping air into my lungs. It was giving me life.

Thank you. Thank you. How could I ever let you know how much I appreciate the help!

Suddenly, I had this amazing lifeline. It was like I was getting a second chance. I had already let one amazing opportunity slip between my fingers, like an idiot, and I was trying to grab it back before it bounced off the ground.

All these people were pitching in, trying to fund my dream, trying to keep it alive. I didn't even know some of them. It was such a boost, knowing that people still believed in me and thought I still had a shot, a big enough shot that they were willing to give me money at a time when they didn't have a ton of it. It was awesome. It was like a shot of adrenaline. It made me want to work harder, push harder. It was definitely an inspiration. But they were also holding me accountable. And one thought was racing through my head: *All these people are invested in this. Invested in me. I can't waste this opportunity. I gotta give it everything I got.*

So, I worked my tail off as a Union Laborer, pouring concrete for Martel Construction in Green Bay, driving back and forth to see Landon several times a week, doing whatever it took.

Then I put in the work off the snow. I trained and weight-lifted and ran like I was getting ready for football season. Josh sold his business in South Carolina. He wanted out and came home for the winter, and I got him into snowboard cross.

We traveled all over the country. He was spending the money that he got from selling his business and his house, making sure that we could get to these races (a favor I would repay down the road, helping him as he chased his dream of starting a new company out west).

For me, the clock was ticking, and the pressure was mounting. I knew all these funds were limited. My friends and family didn't have a lot of money, and I really didn't want to have to ask local businesses for money ever again. There was no telling how long the small businesses in the U.P. could help me. My back was against the wall. I had to produce, and my mindset was fixed:

All of this could be gone in a blink. I gotta keep working, gotta stay focused. The top of one mountain is the bottom of the next. I have to make the team. Not the C team. The A team. I gotta get fully funded. That's the only way to keep doing this. There is really no other option. No room for failure. I can't afford not to make the team.

See the problem, find the answers. You can't do this on your own. You need help. You gotta learn techniques. You gotta study what others are doing. You gotta learn their tricks.

Before the 2006–07 season, I went to Park City, Utah, and started training with Jonathan Cheever. We had known each other for about a year and a half. We met at a team camp in 2005—the first for both of us—and immediately became close friends.

Cheever and I started training together, trying to learn how to turn better. Just putting in the work to become the best snowboarders we could.

We tried to copy Graham Watanabe, who, in my eyes, had the best turning technique. Every time he made a turn it looked picture-perfect. He was so technically sound.

Just by mimicking him, trying to copy his technique, I was improving. But I needed more. I needed a real coach.

So, I started working with Nate Park, who was the head Alpine and Snowboard coach at Copper Mountain.

It was a stroke of good luck for our paths to cross at that point in my career. Years later, Park would coach at Vail, the Olympic Winter Institute in Australia, the Chinese Ski Team and, ultimately, become the U.S. Snowboard Team coach.

The guy knew his stuff.

───────────

"Hey, you gotta grind your snowboard," Park said to me.

"Grind?" I asked. "What the hell is a grind?"

"Really? You don't know what it is?"

"No."

I had just been winging it. Nobody had taught me anything. Nobody had showed me what to do. I was just doing everything on instinct.

"Oh, man; Nick, let me put it in words that you can understand," he said. "It's like you are taking your car into the shop. And we're gonna put a supercharger on it. Then we're gonna give it back to you. That's what I'm going to do to your snowboard."

"Ok," I said. "Sounds good to me. Let's do it."

The more he talked, the more I started to understand it: left untreated, a snowboard formed a natural suction cup to the snow.

"We need to break that suction from the snow," Park said. "And it allows water to kick off and it allows the board to fly way faster."

He took me to this place in Colorado and some guy—actually, a fellow Yooper—put a grind on my snowboard.

I went to X Games, where I was normally qualifying around 18th or 19th. After racing on a board with the proper grind, I qualified second.

It was like a lightbulb had gone off. I had been competing for three or four years against people who were supercharged, and

I didn't even know it. It was like night and day, and it changed everything. It gave me a completely different mindset:

Holy crap! I can make a mistake in a race and still be in it.

When I started doing this sport, I was such an outsider that I didn't know what I didn't know. I didn't know any professional snowboarders. I didn't know crap. I just watched X Games on TV, went online, and started showing up: *Here I am. I don't know what the hell I'm doing, but here I am.*

I didn't use a "grind" in the 2005 or 2006 X Games.

But I did in 2007.

That change, alone, catapulted my career. Gaining that knowledge, alone, from Park made him the best snowboard coach I'd ever had up to that point. Just by him giving me that single tip.

But he also started teaching me how to improve my turning.

I could see that Watanabe was great at turning. But Nate explained it to me, breaking down the reasons why he was so good. Suddenly, with just a little bit more understanding and knowledge, my technique started to improve.

Finally, my snowboard was prepared the right way, setting me up for something amazing.

––––––––

February 2007
Tamarack Resort, Idaho
Final Event of U.S. Snowboard Grand Prix

Cheever and I drove up to Tamarack for the U.S. Grand Prix, which was also the Visa U.S. Nationals. Cheever found a house to rent for a group of us, so we had a good spot. The night before the finals, the owner's kids showed up. They stayed there and threw a party. It turned into an absolute shitshow, so we packed up in the middle of the night and left. We crashed with some friends, sleeping on the floor of their hotel room. Not exactly the ideal setup to try and be competitive for the race.

The next day, seven inches of fresh snow made the roads treacherous and turned the course into a slow-motion battle. The field of 32 was cut down to four in the final…and I was still alive.

Nate Park had a wax overlay that he put on my snowboard, and he said it was perfect for the conditions. It made my board so fast and definitely gave me a tremendous competitive advantage.

In the finals, I beat Austria's Markus Schairer and clinched the U.S. title.

"It was slow today, but I just had to get the right mix on my board," I told Jesse Zentz, a reporter from the *Idaho Statesman*. "When it started snowing, we didn't do anything to the board and it was running fast. The win is just amazing."

It shocked everybody when I won that race. But I was developing. I was learning to calm down and not be so crazy. When I started competing, I approached every race like a football game. Like a gunner on a kickoff, running around, trying to rip people's heads off. But that doesn't work on a snowboard. I learned I could still be aggressive, but I had to be smarter about it, with more thought and finesse. And my style was changing.

Sure, I still made big mistakes. But I was starting to figure it out. Starting to understand what could happen on the course. Starting to understand how to handle the speed and different situations. I was becoming more methodical.

But I also had to give credit to Park. He had waxed my board, and I wouldn't have won if he didn't do that.

Not only did I win the national championship, but I got $10,000 for doing it. It was money I desperately needed. But it was also validation.

———————

In early February, I competed in my first North American Cup in Colorado. If I placed seventh or better, I would get invited to the World Cup in Japan.

How freakin' amazing would that be?

Well, I ended up taking third, which was amazing, and I got the invite. I was so stoked. The bad news? The Japan race was just two weeks away, and I didn't have enough money to get there. I hadn't gotten my $10,000 yet—it took a while to get paid—and my parents didn't have money like that. My mom told my aunt Regina about my predicament, and she was like, "No, you are going."

She forked over the money and bought me a ticket to go to Japan.

Amazing. How could I ever thank you enough?

So many amazing people were helping open the door for me.

February 2007
Furano, Japan
FIS World Cup

We got to Japan and showed up at our hotel, which was giant and really nice. It had this big open ballroom area and the food was spread out—so much food. King crab, all kinds of sushi, every kind of food you can imagine. They had these huge tubs of sake, and I'd get up and fill my sake box. There was this traditional Japanese band, and these people were marching around—*boom, boom, boom*—beating drums. Just the coolest thing. Heck, two French girls dragged me into the girls' bathroom to kiss them.

Oh, my God; this is awesome. This is what I have been missing? This is great.

The weather was great, too. It started dumping snow before the race—more powder than I had ever seen. Powder days weren't really a thing in the Upper Peninsula. My local mountain didn't have enough vertical to make it epic when it snowed. But on this mountain, there was so much snow, and we got to ride powder for two days.

It was the best riding I had ever done in my life. For two days, we were the only people riding in the woods and had untouched powder both days. We would duck the ropes and just ride. People would be yelling from the chair lift and the ski patrol wouldn't follow us into the woods. It was bizarre. I was told that in Japanese culture, the locals wouldn't go in the woods while it was snowing because that was when evil spirits would come out of the woods. OK. That was pretty wild, but we sure as heck went in there and tried to scare them out.

———————————

On race day, I made a huge mistake.

They had one board race ready, ready to rip, fast as heck. But I took the wrong board up to the top, and the wax wasn't even scraped.

The wax tech, Andy Buckley, did what he could. He took all the wax off and he made it work. So, in my first International World Cup, I ended up finishing 10th, which was very good for just coming in and not really knowing what I was doing.

And for, um, using the wrong board.

Best of all, I had avoided the evil spirits coming out of the woods.

———————————

I loved racing in Japan. We had a huge party at the hotel. There was an enormous staircase that wrapped around the lobby where we were partying. I was pushing the Canadian tech, J.P., down the stairs in a baby-changing station of some sort. We were racing luggage carts down the stairs. I think J.P. was having a good time. He grabbed the fire extinguisher off the wall and sprayed it. But we haven't been back to Japan for a long time. The reason was simple: we soon wore out our welcome. When we went to Japan, all the athletes from all the countries would just get crazy. And they would party too hard.

––––––––––––

Some moments shape your life forever, and my year without funding taught me so many lessons. I was pushed to the brink and came out fighting. I learned how to bounce back and never give up. I learned lessons that I would need for the rest of my career.

And if I needed to search through the Yellow Pages to get support, I would do it. But it also showed me, once again, the generosity of Yoopers. Just amazing. They were on this journey with me. They were helping me keep it going—small businesses, some relatives, some strangers—just funding this dream. Amazing.

As far as Japan, I thought every trip was gonna be like that. Amazing powder and crazy parties. French girls trying to kiss me. Firing off fire extinguishers. But I would soon learn they're not. That was, by far, the exception.

CHAPTER 7

"A DIFFERENT BREED"

March 2, 2008
Whiteface Mountain, New York
U.S. Snowboarding Cup

Four of my buddies picked me up and carried me across the snow, heading toward the stage. Two of them put me on their shoulders and the other two lagged behind, just in case I fell backward.

"From the United States of America!" the announcer screamed into the microphone.

I was pumping my fist.

"Nick! BAUMGARTNER!"

They carried me through the crowd and put me on the stage. I turned and pumped my fist after winning the U.S. Snowboarding Cup at Whiteface Mountain. Somebody handed me my snowboard and I lifted it up. There were whistles and screams. What a wild day. I had to ride an additional heat because a rerun was declared in the semifinal. No matter. That didn't bother me. I had been riding fast all season. I was still working on my turns, still learning this sport. But I was getting better. Figuring it out. Learning how to win—I did the same pass four heats in a row and won the Air Force Pass of the Race, which was badass.

"The East Coast is pretty wild, because I'm from the Midwest and the conditions are the same—cold and icy all the time," I said in a video interview put on YouTube by U.S. Snowboarding. "So, it was good. I had a good time."

"What does this victory mean to you?" I was asked.

"Oh," I said, shaking my head. "This victory means so much for me. I'm just glad I can do it. To win the World Cup here and get the national championship in the same race?"

I shook my head

"Man, it's unbelievable."

Just one year after getting cut from the C team, my career was taking off.

So, we did the logical thing. The only thing that seemed right. A couple of my high school buddies and I went to Jamaica, mon— to celebrate the win and relax.

———————

Home Depot put together an amazing program for Olympic athletes. From 1990 through 2008, Home Depot sponsored more than 600 athletes and para-athletes. And the results were hard to ignore. Home Depot Olympic athletes won 18 medals at the 2002 Games in Salt Lake City, Utah, and 10 medals in Torino, Italy, at the 2006 Olympics.

As soon as I met the criteria for the program, I immediately signed up and was accepted.

Home Depot paid an athlete a full year's salary, but the athlete only had to work part-time. All my friends had done it, or they were currently doing it, and they figured it out. A lot of people would trick the system and not do much work that first year, just go in every once in a while. Then, the second year, you needed to really make an effort and put in at least 500 hours of work.

In the Upper Peninsula, the closest Home Depot to my hometown was in Iron Mountain, so I'd commute 45 minutes to the store. I was an associate in the hardware department. Shoppers would come in and say, *Hey, we're looking for this or that.*

I would take them around, show them where products were, and that kind of stuff. And I thought that was stupid. I thought I should have been the greeter at the front of the store. I was very talkative. Good with people. But they just put me in hardware. Oh, well; it was fun. I got to talk to people, I didn't have to do a lot of work, and I got a full year's salary, which was pretty badass.

Home Depot did commercials with some of the athletes, but I never did one. The managers at my store actually wanted me to keep the whole thing quiet. They told me, "We don't want you to tell anyone, because our workers are going to be mad."

Eventually, some of the workers did find out that I was barely doing anything, working just 10 hours a week, while getting paid a full-time salary, which made some people jealous.

Can't say I blame them.

Suddenly, I had some extra money for the first time in my life. I could have taken the Home Depot money and invested it. I could have bought a house. I could have done so many different things to set myself up for the future.

But I was a young kid—a young kid who didn't put too much thought into a financial plan—and I decided that I was going to buy a wakeboard boat. I thought that it would give me an advantage on my snowboard because I'd be able to wakeboard all summer.

My plan was to buy a $15,000 boat. And then I found a guy who owned a dealership. He was willing to give me a brand-new boat at cost. So, I got a $42,000 Moomba for $31,000. A great deal, in theory. My local credit union gave me a loan to buy it because I had the proof that I was getting a full salary from Home Depot. The monthly payment was just shy of 600 bucks, and probably just shy of $500 was going to interest.

What a horrible mistake that turned out to be. I didn't have a house. Didn't have a garage to store it in. Heck, I didn't even have a truck to tow the thing. But there I was. I had a beautiful boat.

I thought, *This is gonna help my snowboarding. This is gonna keep me on the podium, winning events.*

I was trying anything to get better. Just throwing darts at a moving target, hoping one of them would stick and make me even better. Josh was back in Iron River, and he had a truck, so that was all covered. Every day during the summer, I would hook up the trailer to his truck, drive the boat two miles down to Sunset Lake, drop the boat in, wakeboard, and then load the boat back up onto the trailer, drive it back, and park it in the yard across the street at my parents' house in Iron River. And that was what we did every day.

The whole time, I had this crazy idea that this was going to make me a better snowboarder, which, in hindsight, was kind of ridiculous.

––––––––––

After the first year, I realized the boat had been a bad idea, and I tried to sell it.

But nobody bought it. And I spent the whole winter season, which is most of the year in the Upper Peninsula, paying interest on something I couldn't even use.

What a horrible investment. What a mistake.

I thought wakeboarding was going to help my snowboarding. But it turned out the better I got at wakeboarding, the more it hurt my snowboarding, because I learned how to jump farther. Eventually, I started out-jumping the wake...and water is not soft.

In fall 2009, I was still wakeboarding, thinking it was helping. I was warming up and did a side roll, where you kind of flip over the wake. But I overshot the wake and landed out in the flats on my front foot. My front foot went right through the toehole of the bindings, and I messed it up pretty bad.

UGH! What the hell did I just do?

So I went to get an MRI.

"Don't read it," I told them.

Because that would have cost more money.

"I'm gonna send that to my team doctor," I said.

They put the images on a CD. Rather than send it out right away, I didn't even have it read. I started my snowboard season, even though my foot was killing me.

I was afraid of finding out that something was seriously wrong.

I taped up my foot every day before I went out for training. In September, we went to South America and did the first races of the Olympic qualifiers.

The first qualifier was in Chapelco, Argentina, and I got through it by taping my foot, finishing 11th.

Then we went back home. In December, we had a training camp before going to our second qualifier in Telluride, where I took ninth.

I was still taping my foot because it was still pretty painful.

Then, we went to Bad Gastein, Austria, for the third qualifier on January 10—and I took eighth. Five days later, we went to Veysonnaz, Switzerland, for the next qualifier.

Nate Holland, one of my teammates, shoved me off course, making me almost miss a gate, which would have disqualified me. Luckily, I kept my balance enough to get back on course, eliminating Holland from the competition. We had some words at the bottom. I wanted to beat his ass, but I had qualified for the semifinals. He was out, so I let him know that he couldn't stop me, and I jumped on the snowmobile to head back for the next heat. I told one of our coaches what had happened and let them know I wasn't happy. They had words with Nate. I can't imagine someone not getting thrown out, or not getting some kind of punishment from the team, in any other sport. I was so mad, but it also made me want it even more.

Maybe that propelled me onto the podium. I finished third behind France's Pierre Vaultier, who won gold, and Germany's David Speiser, who took silver.

January 21, 2010
Quebec, Canada
World Cup

Finally, my foot stopped hurting. I was in the mix for one of four spots on the 2010 U.S. Olympic team. I was right on the edge of making it, heading into a qualifier at Stoneham Mountain Resort in Quebec.

I was fighting two other snowboarders for the spot. One was Shaun Palmer. I mean, we're talking about the guy who invented this sport, and he was the reason I got into it, watching him crush it at X Games.

The other was Ross Powers, the gold medalist at the 2002 Olympics in halfpipe. He was just an insane snowboarder and the face of halfpipe for years. He crushed it and then decided to make a run at boardercross. The wild thing? The first race that I ever did, the one in Mammoth, California, I raced on his halfpipe pro model snowboard.

Basically, I was trying to get to the Olympics by going up against two legends in the sport. The coaches would pick the team using a complex set of criteria, much of it based on the World Cup finishes. I knew that if I finished high, I would lock up my spot. But in the first heat, a Canadian kid made a mistake and ended up taking me out right at the start.

I finished 11th.

My day was over, and there was nothing I could do. When I got to the bottom, I threw a little hissy fit. A childlike temper tantrum. I freaked out because my spot on the Olympic team was suddenly in jeopardy. I felt helpless—there was nothing I could do to better my spot—and I chucked my board in disgust. I just lost my shit.

The coaches scolded me: "Hey, you cannot do that anymore. It doesn't matter. That's not good."

That scared me.

Was that temper tantrum going to cost me a spot on the Olympic team?

Could the coaches say, *You're not going because you were acting like a fool?*

I was still crying and very emotional at the bottom of the course, and Palmer and Powers were the only two that could bump me. But Powers missed it by one place. He finished in ninth.

That left Palmer. He ended up going all the way to the big final, and if he got first or second, he would get the spot to go to the Olympics. Graham Watanabe was in that final race and he had already locked up his spot on the Olympic squad. He could have just thrown the race and let Palmer beat him, which would have given Palmer the spot on the Olympic team. But luckily for me, Graham was a competitor, as fair as they come. He was an amazing, good guy. He talked with the coaches and asked them, "What should I do?" And they said, "You do what you do. You go out there and you try to win this."

If it would have been one of our other teammates, like Nate Holland, I know he would have let Palmer win to knock me out for sure, just because they were better friends. They're from the same area, and Nate didn't really like me.

But Watanabe went for it and finished second—and more importantly for me, Palmer ended up third. That gave me the final spot.

I was named to the U.S. Olympic Team for the Vancouver Games, along with defending gold medalist Seth Wescott, Holland, and Watanabe. It was a huge relief. I was 28 years old, heading to my first Olympic Games.

My mom, Mary, sent an email to dozens of family members and friends telling them the news.

January 2010
Aspen, Colorado
Winter X Games

At X Games, I finally handed the CD with the MRI images of my foot to Dr. Tom Hackett, our team doctor. He looked at it and was stunned. "Oh, my God, Nick; you got to be kidding me," he said.

My whole arch bone—the middle of my foot, whatever that thing was called—was shattered. It looked like it had these spider cracks through the whole bone.

"Well, it doesn't hurt anymore," I said.

"You got so lucky," Hackett said. "It must have healed, and you're fine. You're lucky something really bad didn't happen."

———————

When I left for the 2010 Winter Olympics, I got the most amazing gift, Yooper-style. A sendoff that lasted several days and turned into a 70-mile parade from Michigan to Wisconsin.

It started with a pep rally at West Iron County High School. My high school.

Landon was just five years old, and his kindergarten class appeared, holding cards with letters written on them. When it was Landon's turn to speak, he said, "L is for Landon, and I'm so proud he's my dad."

The children unscrambled the letters and it read: "We love Nick."

Just about broke my heart. That night, I was escorted around town on the front bumper of a fire truck. My mom was crying, and it was unbelievable. We were trying to raise money by selling T-shirts that read POWERED BY THE UP on the front. On the back, they read, PLAY HARD. DREAM BIG.

A slogan that basically summed up my life.

Three days later, we had an amazing parade to the Green Bay airport. From Iron River to Crystal Falls into Wisconsin through Florence and Spread Eagle and Iron Mountain…all these people, wishing me good luck. Yooper-style.

It said so much about my hometown. So much about the people who lived in the Upper Peninsula and Wisconsin. Where I'm from, when something good happens, everyone celebrated it. Everyone felt good for each other. Everybody rooted for each other.

February 2010
Vancouver, Canada
2010 Winter Olympics

We flew to West Vancouver, British Columbia, and we went to a press conference before our event. The entire U.S. team sat in front of the media, and I realized they had put the wrong nameplate in front of my seat. The incorrect one read: BRUCE BAUMGARTNER.

Bruce Baumgartner was a four-time Olympic medalist in wrestling who retired shortly after the 1996 Atlanta Games.

"Bruce?" I said, looking at it. "Yeah? Well, I wrestled a few years back."

The reporters broke into laughter.

Pre-Olympic press conferences were wild. For one thing, the media always seemed to focus on one central question. But the other weird thing was how they would ask other snowboarders about you—in front of you.

Sure enough, it happened again. "What is Nick like?" a reporter asked Graham Watanabe.

"He's a different breed of snowboard-crosser because he has a different level of energy," Watanabe replied. "It's like when you go to the pet store and get some kind of mutt, but this mutt grows up to be a mastiff with the energy of a puppy. That's Nick."

I had several nicknames: Neck Head, Neck Face, and Baum.

But maybe Watanabe was right. Maybe I was a mutt. An athletic mutt. A guy who was a former college football player, wrestler, and track runner who turned into a snowboarder. And I still had a lot of football player in me. A lot of the wrestler with an aggressive attitude. I got along with everyone, but they knew once the race started, I was not someone they could push out of the way.

When I was asked about my approach for the Olympics, I was direct and honest: "Got to stay focused," I told reporters. "That's why I'm here."

Our U.S. team was stacked. Wescott was the reigning snowboardcross champion; Holland was a five-time X Games champion; Watanabee was a three-time World Cup winner and a 2006 Olympian; and I was the World Champion bronze medalist.

"It was a huge battle to make this men's SBX team," Peter Foley, our coach, told reporters. "Six different U.S. riders have already been on the World Cup podium this season, and only four of them make the Olympic team. We are going into the 2010 Games with one of the strongest lineups possible."

The press conference ended.

And we started going through training runs. One of the big stories was the Canadians' tight snow pants. Nate Holland made sure to bring it up and make it a story.

So the media kept asking us about it.

"We want to keep the cool factor in snowboarding; we don't want it to go to speed suits," I told reporters on Cypress Mountain.

Heck yes, I was ribbing the Canadians.

We were wearing our normal, baggy gear, and they had these skintight, ugly things. It didn't make sense, because there was always a longstanding gentlemen's agreement to keep boarder-crossers in loose-fitting pants.

Thank goodness, we were wearing denim-colored pants. "Little jokes here and there but we all get along pretty well, so it's hard to get too into it because we're all friends," I told reporters. "I'm just stoked about ours, we've got the coolest pants."

I felt so comfortable on this course. I was the fastest qualifier during the previous year's test event at Cypress, and as a Yooper, it was fitting—I felt so comfortable because our uniform was jeans and a flannel.

The uniform of the Upper Peninsula.

I volunteered to wear a helmet cam during the competition. A lot of people didn't want to do it because they thought it was going to slow them down because of aerodynamics. But I agreed to wear it because our sport needed exposure. Our sport needed a boost. I figured any chance we had to bring the fans closer to the action, any opportunity we had to get them on the board with me, they would be hooked.

These Olympics were crazy because all the snow for the jumps and features was flown in via helicopter from Mt. Baker, Washington. They spent $10,000 an hour using one of those huge firefighting helicopters. The entire base where the fans would watch was made of giant hay bales and then covered with snow. The day before the event, all the general admission standing-room-only tickets got canceled because the snow was melting. It had rained for both training days and the snow was a mess.

"You try not to have any nerves and stuff, but this is my first Olympic Games and—I'm not going to lie—there's some nerves that first run," I told reporters. "That second run, I had a blast—I was cruising through the bottom straightaway and I was thinking, 'Yeah! This is how it's supposed to feel.'"

I had the seventh fastest time after qualifying.

Finally, when I got a chance to race, I didn't have a particularly good start in the first run but stayed close and waited for the right time to make my move. As we took a step-down jump into a long straightaway, I went for it, passing two. Following Rob Fagan into the next jump, I had to get out of the main race line to pass and I got bogged down by the loose snow.

I fell trying to clear the next double.

I finished in 20th place, and I was disappointed.

"It's not fun," I told reporters. "I expected to be in the final here, and to go out in the first round, well, that wasn't what I was going for. But it's the nature of the sport, and it's how it played out today."

The standing-room-only section was washed away because of rain. I found my parents, and I heard my brother Robby before I saw him. I just listened for his duck and goose calls. He was dressed in his hunting camo.

Wescott ended up winning his second gold medal.

And I vowed to keep going.

"I'll be in Sochi," I told reporters, referring to the 2014 Winter Games in Russia.

But first, I enjoyed every second of Vancouver.

———————

One of the coolest parts of the Olympics was getting the chance to watch other sports. I went to a U.S. hockey game and met Ken Yaffe, an NHL executive, and he decided I needed to come to every game and watch from their suite.

So every day I'd wake up, eat breakfast, then head to the hockey rink and hang out with Yaffe and Brendan Shanahan, the former Red Wing who had retired, to watch the game in the NHL suite. After the first game, we'd walk to the House of Hockey to eat along with Shanahan's friend Will Arnett, the actor and comedian. Then we'd head back to the rink for the second game. I think I met every single famous person that came to the Games: Michael J. Fox, Seth Rogen, Michael Phelps, Jason Bateman, and several NHL team owners.

I'd head back to the Olympic Village to shower and eat and then head out to meet them again. Then, it started to get wild. We'd party at some of the coolest places until 5 AM. I would sleep until 11, then head back to the rink to do it all over again.

One of the best parties was in a penthouse suite, where I met Wayne Gretzky and his wife, his son, Ty, and daughter, Paulina, along with their friends Alyonka and Diana Larionov, the daughters of former Red Wing Igor Larionov.

After the party, Wayne sent us all off in a limo to go have fun. We went from party to party, going straight to the VIP area every time. At one point, NHL superstar Alexander Ovechkin came up to us with a huge tray of shots, and I had a shot with him.

It blew me away.

Just crazy, that a small-town kid from the U.P. was hanging with people like this.

After the Olympics, they decided to take the entire Olympic team to the Junior World Championships in New Zealand. We were all there to help the kids and to coach them. They also thought it was important for us do things that got us out of our comfort zone, to be comfortable being uncomfortable. So, they actually took us bungee jumping. In New Zealand, the home of bungee jumping.

We went to this one station where the jump was 150 or 160 feet, and you normally jumped down and dipped into the river. But there was a log hung up just upriver, so they couldn't let us dip into the river.

So, I did that.

On another day, we moved on to a 300-meter cannon swing. On the way there, I remember being nervous. We were going to jump off a ledge. "Man, I hope there is a river down there so that I'm not nervous in case something happens," I said.

Then, we got ready for a 449-foot bungee jump with an 8.5-second free fall. Just crazy. When they strapped the bungee on me, and they did it all quick—zip, zip. Just velcro.

I was thinking, *Oh, crap; that went too quick.*

"Whoa," I said. "Whoa—are we sure you did that right?"

"You got this," they said.

They stood me up and I could barely move my feet. Just four or five inches at a time, I waddled out to this platform.

My coach looked down and said, "Hey, Baum, there's your river down there."

It was just these huge monster rocks with this little creek that was trickling through it. I was thinking: *All right now, just do it. Don't be wimpy; just do it.*

Three…two…one!

I jumped. Kind of a half jump. More of a fall. Then, all these emotions went through my head.

One: *I can't believe I just jumped!*

Then: *Ah, sick, this is the most awesome thing I've ever done!*

Then: *Oh, my God, when is that cord gonna start stretching? Start stretching.*

START STRETCHING!

And then I bounced a couple times: *Woo!* Whew!

Amazing.

I loved doing things to keep me on the edge. Because my sport demanded it. Learning how to handle crazy situations, learning how to face fears and still go through with it—that was the essence of my sport.

So, we were helping the kids, helping coach them, but it was kind of a reward and celebration—*Hey, you guys; great job. Way to put in the hard work.*

Rather than flying straight home, we made a stop in Fiji, because it really didn't cost any extra money.

We went to the beach and got to surf for a week, which was unbelievable.

Hey, I'm only doing this to become a better snowboarder! Ha!

I had only gone surfing a few times. The first time was in Chile. I didn't even know how to pick out a surfboard, but we went and rented boards. I picked out one that was small and sporty and fast, not knowing that I didn't know what I was doing. So, we went to the spot to surf, and it was so big and so scary. We had to jump out and paddle as quick as possible to get outside of these rocks, and it didn't take long to get washed away like a mile down the beach.

But in Fiji I was so much better than when I was in Chile. I felt a little bit more comfortable. I had the right board; we had the right crew; and it was just a lot more fun. I still got pummeled and smashed by waves, but I was learning how to do it. I always told people that when you surf and you catch a wave for the first time, it's the most amazing feeling ever, because you probably almost died about seven times before you got that wave. Catching that first wave was so amazing because it was like you conquered mother nature and were riding on her back. Such a moment of freedom.

Every morning, we'd get up and walk to the docks, jump on a boat, and drive five to 10 miles out into the ocean. Some mornings, we'd see whales and dolphins, just cruising out there. Then we went to the most beautiful blue water. It was incredible to be able to learn how to surf—and to do that with somebody like Seth Wescott, who had just won a gold medal? Incredible.

I remember sitting in the boat taking a break from snorkeling.

"Shark!" Lindsey Jacobellis screamed.

I rushed to the back of the boat, grabbed my mask, and dived in, struggling to put the mask on. I wasn't nervous, because it was so clear and reef sharks are not particularly aggressive unless provoked.

I saw a small one.

When people asked me, "Oh, do you surf?"

I always said, "Well, I wouldn't consider myself a surfer. But I've surfed in Chile and in Fiji in some of the most beautiful water and the best waves in the world."

Sometimes I would think about how things worked out.

What would have happened if I had sent Dr. Hackett that CD earlier? What if he had diagnosed the injury when it was hurting?

Would they have held me out for the beginning of the season? Would I have missed a chance to be in the 2010 Olympics?

Wakeboarding for two summers almost ruined my chances at making the 2010 Olympic team.

Then, I wouldn't have gone to New Zeeland. Wouldn't have gone bungee jumping. Wouldn't have surfed in Fiji.

It's just wild how life turns out. But there's something else—it was a good thing that I'm a procrastinator. Ha!

March 23, 2010
Barcelona, Spain

We were in Barcelona, hanging out, and we decided to rent some scooters. Holy crap—you want to talk about loose. Get a bunch of young adults from the U.S. and let them rent scooters.

We were at stoplights, shooting through the cars. I went with a couple of guys to ride our scooters down this trail. We got to the end, and everybody started turning their scooters around all nice and easy. On this really skinny goat path—forward and back, forward and back, forward and back.

"That's not how you do it, guys," I said.

I laid this scooter down and gassed it. It spun right around my legs, and I stood it back up.

I was thinking, *Look how sick I am!*

But when I stood it back up, it jumped forward a little bit. I whiskey-throttled it, and I launched off this goat path, careening 20 feet down a steep hill into a huge pricker bush.

No, no, no!

Just brutal.

But it was almost inevitable…when you let grown children rent scooters.

How no one died, I have no idea.

We drove the scooters all over Barcelona. Then we decided to drive all the way up the Tibidabo Hill to the Torre De Collserola, a famous tower. We got up to this high point in the city and stopped at a cool lookout to take a break.

On the way down, I was driving like an idiot, popping wheelies at every stoplight, weaving through traffic. For some reason, I thought it was a good idea to stand up on my scooter and spread my arms out like an airplane. Unfortunately, there was a cop just down the hill and he waved us all down—nearly 10 scooters in a single-file line.

He waved everybody through until he got to me. He flagged me off to the side and then let the rest of them go. He started screaming at me in Spanish.

"Sorry," I said. "No Spanish."

Like a dumb American tourist.

His partner walked up and spoke English. "No problem—I got this," he said. "This is a public street, not the *Titanic*."

I was doing my best to talk my way out of a ticket.

Graham Watanabe, my teammate, walked up while doing a terrible job hiding his Go Pro. That just ticked off the cops even more. Guaranteed, I was getting a ticket.

"Get out of here," I yelled at Watanabe.

Then, something crossed my mind: *I know I'm getting a ticket. Easy; I just won't pay it. I'm from the U.S. I'm sure it won't ever come up again.*

Then, they pulled out a credit card machine and made me pay $450 on the spot. But at least the two cops let me take a picture, holding the ticket, standing between them. I was wearing a RIGHT TO PLAY sweatshirt that I had gotten in Vancouver from the owner of Roots Clothing. Right To Play is an amazing charity to help kids all around the world get access to sports. But in this case, the shirt made a great joke, because I had no right to play *Titanic* on their streets.

In 2011, I thought that I was a lock to be put on the world championship team to go to Spain. But we only had four spots, and nothing was certain. We were in a meeting and Shaun Palmer chirped up: "You should take Alex Deibold instead of Baumgartner to give someone else a try."

Palmer was still pretty ticked that they took me to the Olympics rather than him. Palmer was a competitor, and our relationship definitely changed after that. I understand with his history why he was upset, but the coaches went strictly off of our results, keeping it fair. The coaches ending up coming to me the next day and telling me that they were taking Deibold. I had mixed feelings. Part of me was incredibly upset. I was thinking, *That's my spot. I earned it. What is going on? This isn't fair.*

But I saw the other side, too. I was friends with Deibold. He was a good buddy of mine. Did he deserve an opportunity? He absolutely did. So I didn't flip out. I didn't freak out, even though I wanted to. I decided to change my focus and keep training for X Games, just two weeks away.

This X Games meant so much to me because it was the first time that Landon was going to see me race in person. He was six years old and I was so excited. After not making the world championship team, I created a master plan: *I'm gonna put in a bunch of work, get better, get even faster, and then when the U.S. team comes back from Worlds, I'm gonna win X Games and show them they made the wrong decision. I won't say a word. I won't have to. They'll know they picked the wrong person. I'll prove it on the snow.*

On the second day of training at Copper Mountain, I doubled into the corner. I overshoot it, flew up the berm—to me, it felt like I was 10 to 15 feet in the air, although I'm not sure—and I ended up in the fence. I crashed on my shoulder and it was extremely painful. I couldn't believe it. Just 12 days from the X Games.

Shaun Palmer came up to me as I was lying on the side of the mountain, and he was like, "What's up, man? How are you feeling?"

"My shoulder," I said, showing him the area that hurt.

"It's broken," he said. "I've done that a few times."

"No!" I couldn't believe it. "No!"

I was so bummed out. "I gotta race. I can't miss X Games. Landon is coming."

X-rays confirmed that my collarbone was broken, so I called Dr. Tom Hackett, our team physician.

"Hey, I need your help," I said.

"What's up?" he said.

"I broke my collarbone and X Games are next week," I said. "Landon is coming for the first time. I got to race."

"All right, do me a favor," Hackett said. "Find somebody who can take a picture of your X-rays and send it to me."

I was at a dark restaurant. I got my X-ray, held it up to the kitchen window, and took a picture of it and sent it to him. This time, I didn't procrastinate like an idiot.

"Be in my office at 10 tomorrow morning in Vail," he said.

So, the next day I drove to the hospital, and he put 15 screws and a plate in my shoulder to hold it all together.

"I made you Bomb-proof," he joked. Baum was my nickname, so I thought that was pretty funny.

This was all so new to me. I had never broken a bone in my life. Some of it was luck—knock on wood. But I had always had a strong frame and I always stayed fit, in part so that I wouldn't get injured.

I wasn't quite sure how to handle an injury like this. I couldn't just tape this up and go out and race, like I did with my foot. I had planned to train for a week, getting ready for X Games. But Dr. Hackett told me to sit on my couch and do nothing. My shoulder was beat up, I was in a lot of pain, but I didn't take painkillers. I've never been a big fan of painkillers, because they mask the pain and actually put you in danger of injuring yourself even more. Since I was in Colorado, I had a friend get me some edibles—because opioids are so addictive—and I sat on a couch for the whole week, trying to rest up and recover quickly.

Nine days after surgery, I showed up at X Games with Dr. Hackett because he was a consultant for the competition. He took care of all our athletes.

"I'm gonna make sure they don't tell you 'no,'" he told me.

I was determined to race, even with an injured collarbone.

"You do need to understand that if you crash, it's gonna be gnarly," Dr. Hackett said. "It'll be another surgery. But longer."

"No, it won't," I said.

"Nick, I guarantee you it will," he said. "Trust me."

"It won't," I argued. "I'm still gonna go to sleep. And when I wake up, this is going to be fixed. It's gonna be longer for you, but it ain't gonna be any different for me."

I started laughing.

I showed up at X Games with my arm in a sling.

"What did you do?" Sarah Castaneda, an organizer, asked.

"I'm here to race," I said.

"All right," she said. "As soon as you get done with registration, we're gonna need you to go over to medical and check in with them."

Dr. Hackett went in with me.

"How does it feel?" I was asked.

"It feels pretty good," I lied.

Dr. Hackett explained what he did.

"Well, can you do a push-up?" one of the medical staff asked me.

"Of course I can," I said, unsure if I could.

I jumped on the ground and did push-ups. I didn't show any emotion, but it hurt like heck. And they let me enter the race.

Nine days after the surgery, I was on the course.

I was under strict doctor's orders to ease into it and not to hit the big jump at the bottom. So, I went out there and did what I was told. I definitely took it easy.

I was going to be fine, as long as I didn't fall. Of course, *not falling* preparing for a snowboarding competition was nearly impossible.

Actually, on the inspection run, I was messing around, and I jumped up and slid on my board and I kind of fell backward. I put my arm out to catch myself. As soon as it touched the snow, pain shot through my upper body and a voice screamed through my head: *No, no, no, no, no, no, no! Don't do that. Don't do that.*

"Nick," one of my coaches said. "There's no way you're going to be able to train, qualify, and race without falling. It just doesn't happen."

"Well, I'm gonna try," I said.

On the second day, I was allowed to hit the big jump—99 feet to the knuckle.

When you overshoot it, which we were doing in the race, we were jumping 130 feet. So here I was, 10 days post-surgery, and I had to hit a jump of more than 100 feet on my snowboard at 60 miles an hour.

So, I grabbed my buddy Alex Deibold—the guy they selected for the world championships instead of me.

"Hey, can I follow you?" I asked him.

I needed to use somebody to judge the speed.

"Absolutely," he said. "Follow me. Just understand when you come over the crest, coming down to that last jump, you can't do a speed check; you need every bit of speed you can get just to clear it."

"Okay, yeah, no problem," I said.

Halfway through the course, there was this cool feature called a butter box. You jumped up and there was this huge gap. I don't know the distance, but it was freakin' nuts.

Alex ate it on top of the butter box, crashing to the snow, so I just kept going. I was going alone without anybody to help me judge my speed. I went through the rest of the course only thinking about the last jump, just going through the motions, thinking it through and concentrating: *Don't speed check, don't speed check, don't speed check.*

I came to the crest and immediately slid sideways, slowing down. *No, no, no! You can't!*

I tucked as low as I could to try to gain as much speed as possible. I came over that spot and popped off the jump as hard as I possibly could, clearing that jump by about an inch, maybe an inch and a half, at a place where five people had bruised their heels, one person shattered his foot, and my buddy from Canada said, "Ah, hell no!" and quit racing for good.

If you came up short when you were going 60 miles an hour, jumping 100 feet, bad things would happen.

So, I was able to make it over that, and then I went through qualifying the next day. I was being cautious, taking it easy. Just trying to get through. I qualified toward the back. That was fine. I just needed to advance.

So, I got into race day. And I think I learned a little bit about myself on that day. I wasn't worried about winning. I was thinking, *You are just lucky to be competing. Just enjoy it. And put on a show for Landon.*

At least, that was my goal. Just to get to this moment. Just to get to the bottom without crashing. I wasn't freaking out, putting pressure on myself to finish in a certain place.

Before the first heat, because my qualifying run was so bad, I got whatever lane was leftover. I was joking around. "Yeah, that's the one I want!"

Everybody was saying, "No shit you want that one, that's all that's left."

I was just having a good time.

"This is so sick," I said.

I was having so much fun, just being there, not worried about my shoulder, and I was riding fast. I not only made it through the first heat, but I had the fastest start and beat everybody to the bottom.

Heat two? Same thing. I got the last pick and ended up with a subpar lane. The crappy one. The one everybody thought was the slowest. Again, I was able to win the hole shot, ride fast, and win again.

At the bottom, I saw Landon and waved to him and everybody was cheering. It was just a huge crowd.

We went back up to the top and I was thinking, *All right, dude, I'm in the finals. First time I've been in the finals of the X Games. Here we go. Let's have some fun.*

Before the final, I got the same crappy lane that nobody wanted. I took off and I was gone. Just flying. I was probably 50 feet in front by the end of the first straightaway. Then there was a section in the middle, called the slipstream, where it didn't matter how far ahead you were; they were gonna draft, and they were gonna catch you. So, they drafted and caught up. Just as I expected.

I made a mistake on one of the rollers, leaving a little room.

Kevin Hill, a Canadian, passed me and I fell into second. Nate Holland, who had won the previous five years, was hot on my tail. But I dived in and stayed behind Hill. We went through these next sections, and I was just staying close, right behind Hill. We went off a jump, and Hill jumped in, going left to set up the next turn. I tucked down low to my board, heading straight into the corner. No setup. I was on his tail now. As soon as I came through that corner, we went up and over that spot where I wasn't supposed to speed check.

Out of the draft now, I pointed my board straight and shot into the lead.

I took the jump, soaring into the air, looking like a cat flying out of a window, swinging my arms even with a broken collarbone, just to keep my body straight. When you go that fast on a snowboard, the wind wants to turn you sideways.

I landed smooth and dragged my back hand on the ground, doing a wheelie and pointing my board out across the finish line.

I had won X Games.

Twelve days after surgery.

As far as I could remember, it was the first competition in my career where I went through the whole event without falling—not in training, not in qualifying, and not during the races.

I had learned an important lesson. *The key is staying loose. Don't be worried about going out there and killing everybody. Just have fun. Just enjoy it.*

I got my board off as fast as possible and sprinted straight to my son. I grabbed Landon and lifted him over my head, carrying him out in front of the cameras.

Heck no, I wasn't feeling any pain. I was only feeling this surge of incredible pride and joy, seeing how much fun Landon was having. It was amazing. I took Landon up on the podium with me so they could put the medal around his neck, and I sent him back to elementary school a rock star. Even though he was still young, hopefully he had learned an important lesson that day. I wanted him to see that if you make a crazy outlandish goal and bust your butt and don't give up when life knocks you down or gives you incredible challenges, like a broken collarbone, it was possible to accomplish anything.

Being a parent had changed me and how I looked at things. But I was also under pressure to provide for him.

Thankfully, I won $25,000, which was crazy money for me. The sense of accomplishment was incredible. I had won X Games, the one giant goal that I had made when I started this crazy journey in 2002. Back then, snowboard cross wasn't in the Olympics. X Games *was* our Olympics.

To see the look in Landon's eyes, to see how proud he was, to see his excitement…man, it was the greatest feeling ever.

CHAPTER 8

TRUCKS, CRASHES, AND A BILLIONAIRE

TRUCKS AND BOARDS.

Nothin' better.

Growing up watching X Games on ESPN, I saw several athletes make a name for themselves in one extreme sport and then use that platform to cross over to auto racing.

Bucky Lasek won 10 X Games gold medals in skateboarding, and he became a rallycross driver.

Travis Pastrana fascinated me. He was involved in everything from supercross and motocross to freestyle motocross and rally racing. Winning X Games, doing a little bit of everything.

And I was in Aspen when Brian Deegan won gold in Moto X Best Trick. He transitioned to four wheels and I used to watch him race trucks. At a race in Las Vegas, he asked me to rep the Metal Mulisha—a clothing line he cofounded—and I did at the 2012 Winter X Games, when I won the silver medal.

Just getting to meet people like that...how insane for a small-town kid.

All of these guys had a heck of a life, and they were showing me what was possible.

That's what I wanna do. I wanna race trucks. I wanna race against these guys, that would be sick.

So, when I started the whole snowboard thing, chasing one dream, I always had another one in the back of my mind, hoping to make a name for myself in snowboarding, cross over, and try to race rally cars. Like Pastrana and Lasek and Deegan.

It just happened that there was a big truck racing scene in the Midwest. Two of the biggest tracks, the most renowned tracks in the country, were each within an hour or an hour and a half from my house.

Chris Bowser, a friend, started racing trucks just by chance, and he said, "Hey, you should come and talk to me on the radio and be my spotter."

I jumped at it: "Heck yeah."

Turned out, I sucked at it.

To be a good spotter, you needed to stay calm and remain measured, and I was none of those things. I went to a race and started yelling at him.

But I had gotten the bug and I began wondering, *What the hell am I doing on the sidelines, telling him how to race? I need to be in that truck!*

Chris was looking to sell one of his trucks so he could focus on racing in a bigger class. He had people interested in buying his truck, but I urged him to wait and let me figure out a way to make it happen financially. I asked him to give me a month and see if I could come up with the money.

Thankfully, he understood how passionate I was, and he waited.

A couple of years earlier, I had bought a house in Iron River, and I was afraid that I couldn't afford a race truck. To begin with, I didn't make a lot of money as a professional snowboarder.

So, I did a little home improvement. I refinanced my house and took $10,000 out to make improvements on it—in theory.

I actually used that money to buy Chris' truck. It wasn't fraud or anything, because I'll tell you what—it had improved my house instantly.

My house is *way cooler* with a race truck in the driveway.

I started competing in TRAXXAS TORC Series off-road, short-course events, and I had a lot of success. Just fell in love with racing. I don't know if it was because I was a better driver than the other guys. But my truck was way better than anything anybody else had. The motor alone was worth $7,000, and some of the trucks that I was racing against, the whole truck and motor cost less than $5,000.

That was my first lesson: when all else fails, always make sure you have the best truck. Gives you a heck of an advantage.

Just like having the best, fastest Oxess snowboards.

I started asking a lot of questions about truck racing, just like when I started snowboarding. I did a lot of research. Tried to get sponsors. Refused to accept "no" for an answer. And started to figure out how to make this work.

Everyone told me the same thing: "If you want to race trucks professionally, if you get serious about this, if you want to meet the right people and find some sponsors, you gotta go to SEMA in Las Vegas."

SEMA—the Specialty Equipment Market Association—held one of the biggest automotive trade shows in the world.

So, I went for it. I got to the show in Vegas and tried to drum up sponsors.

Walking around, meeting people came natural to me.

Selling myself? Selling this dream? That was natural, too. Because I had done it for so long as a snowboarder.

I went up to every single person I could find and gave them my sales pitch, trying to get them to sponsor me. All the other truck racers were walking around, doing the same thing. They said things like, "I race trucks."

Solid. Predictable. But I had something even better in my back pocket.

I went up to those same sponsors and introduced myself to them: "Hey, I race trucks."

I went through the things I had accomplished. I tried to get them excited about my truck racing experience. Tried to sell them on my passion. I tried to explain who I was and what my vision was. Then, I hit them with the hook: "And I am a professional snowboarder."

And they would say, "Wait, what did you say?"

"Yeah, I'm an Olympic snowboarder."

"Really?"

"Yeah."

Wait for it.

"And I just *won* the X Games on ESPN."

They were like, "Wha—what did you say? You gotta come meet this guy."

Inevitably, they would take me over to meet the actual person that I needed to talk to all along, the real decision-maker. If snowboarding taught me anything, it was how to gives a sales pitch to potential sponsors. To stay alive in these sports, I had to learn how to become a salesman. How to pitch myself and my dream and be persistent and creative. But most of all, how to land a deal. I ended up getting a sweet one with Henkel Corporation's Team Loctite.

They were like, *Well, yeah, we want to sponsor you.*

But they only wanted to sponsor my snowboarding. At least, that was where it started.

In January, I took second at X Games. Of course, I was using Loctite threadlocking adhesives, and they were thrilled. I ended up partying in Aspen with Mike Shanahan, who was Henkel's director of marketing for North America. I told him, "Hey, this is awesome, but we need to go truck racing."

He gave me several "No's" over the course of the weekend. But I was persistent. I was a Yooper. And Yoopers refuse to give up.

After I took second, after we went out and partied, after he really got to know me—maybe after he saw how I treated people and how outgoing I was—he changed his tune.

"When you get home, send me a proposal," Shanahan said.

Loctite gave me $120,000 to race in the professional ranks, and they paid this team to allow me to race their trucks for two years.

When I stepped back and realized everything that had happened, I was stunned. In a two-year span, I went from never having raced anything with a motor in it...in my *entire* life...to being in the pro ranks, racing in a truck in a Pro Lite series. And it was so badass; it was just crazy.

My plan was coming together. I had won X Games and was crossing over into racing. It all just happened. Because I made it happen. That's the secret to life. I was persistent and I wasn't afraid to ask anybody to become my sponsor.

So, I started racing. But it took some time to figure it all out. I won all the time at the lower ranks and in lower trucks. But once I moved up to the pro truck tracks, it was a little different story.

And I would make plenty of mistakes along the way.

The first time I ever drove the race truck, I totaled it.

Andy Zipperer, the Infinity Motorsports team owner, allowed me to race his truck, and Loctite paid for it. Andy picked me up and we drove 32 hours to Phoenix, Arizona, to get a taste of racing. It wasn't part of our series, but he wanted me to get a feel for it before we started racing for real. Our first race was going to be in Charlotte, North Carolina, about a month later.

So, we drove 32 hours in a semi with these race trucks. The whole time, he was telling me, "Don't hit the step up, the step up on this track—everyone wrecks their vehicles going into the step up."

A "step up" was a jump where you landed on a spot higher than where you took off. In essence, you were jumping up to a landing spot. Like jumping up to the next step on a stairway.

So I tried to reassure him: *Oh, yeah. For sure.*

But I guess I didn't take him seriously.

I went out for the first practice and did the first turn. The truck biked up on the two wheels and I almost flipped over. I turned to the outside of the corner, making the truck settle back down on all four wheels. Deep breath.

Thought I lost it. Okay, we got through that.

The other thing I heard about these trucks was if you don't drive them hard, with the hammer down, they flipped. So, I was flying around the track, racing the other guys alongside me out there in practice. Just going for it.

First lap: I came around, there was the step up, and I just followed all the trucks and we all hit the step up. Got through it, no problem.

Second lap: We went around, and I hit the step up again. Got through it again.

And I went back around. Later, I was told by the crew that the owner was up in the stands saying, "Holy shit, dude, he's fast right out of the box. This is awesome."

Third lap: I hit the step up, and took this other lane, feeling it out, getting used to maneuvering the truck around the track.

This is sick!

Fourth lap: I came around the corner and went a little bit wider. I was coming up to the step up. But now, I was two truck widths to the left. The jump was a little bit kicky, and I bottomed out the shocks going off the jump. That made the rear end of the truck shoot up in the air and the nose dropped down. I landed on the front of the truck, stabbing the nose into the ground, and it flipped over. I slammed the rear driver's side tire into the ground, basically ripping the rear end out of the truck, bending everything.

Damn, damn, damn.

They picked me up in a wrecker and dragged my truck off the track. I was thinking, *Oh, my God, this owner's gonna be so mad.*

That was on a Friday. We were supposed to race on Saturday and again on Sunday.

So, I started scrambling, trying to put it back together again.

By Sunday, I had talked to all these other truck teams and got everyone to help me. The Geiser Bros., who are big-time and build some of the biggest desert race trucks in the world, had a shop down the road. They picked up some stuff for me and we pieced the truck back together. I got a driveshaft from somebody and this other company fixed the driveshaft. The whole thing cost $100. Hard to believe we were able to fix $10,000 worth of damage for $100.

Or so I thought.

On Sunday morning, I took the truck out. The organization allowed me to do a lap to make sure it was working. I went out there and it started smoking and the temperature was rising on it.

No! No! No!

So, I pulled over. It turned out when I landed on the nose, I had ripped the motor mount right out of the side of the motor. A $19,000 problem. Just that alone. The only fix was a new motor.

So yeah, I went into truck racing with this confidence that came from snowboarding and I went out there, right off the bat, and got humbled so fast.

Yeah, dude, you're not some phenom. You're not gonna come in here and just kick butt.

———————

After destroying that truck, we fixed it up, got a new motor, and continued on to Charlotte, North Carolina. I had learned my lesson. The crash pulled me back a little bit, gave me a lesson in caution, and I went the rest of the year without wrecking anything.

Progress!

Then, something crazy happened. I was on Twitter and I saw that Robby Gordon, who used to race NASCAR, was starting a new series, and he was inviting one of the other drivers who was driving in the same class as me.

I looked up the organization, the Stadium Super Trucks, and I looked at all the people they were inviting, and I realized they were inviting all these X Games athletes, like Brian Deegan, Travis Pastrana, and Bucky Lasek.

I thought, *Hey, I have an X Games gold, and I just took second at the X Games and went to the Olympics; maybe they'll let me race.*

I blindly sent an email to the organizers, telling them my accolades: "Hey, I race Pro Lites. Do you think I can come and test these?"

Natasha Gordon replied to my email and asked, "What kind of tires do you want to run?"

You gotta be shittin' me. This is really gonna happen?

It was the summer of 2012, and I only had a few days to get ready. I hurried up and got a plane ticket and flew to California. I went to the Summer X Games and hung out with the Loctite folks because they were sponsoring some stuff there. I had rented a car and didn't want to spend extra money to get a hotel room, so I slept in the parking garage right next to X Games in my Nissan Xterra rental car. I wanted to make sure that if I was going to get a hotel, it was going to be near everyone else in the organization so that I could build a relationship with these people. So, I drove into the desert to this track. They were planning on two days of testing. They had all these trucks there and all these athletes coming in to drive them.

On the first day, I was a nobody to them, and they were not gonna let me drive.

They were like, "Cool, you're a snowboard guy, cool, whatever. You drive Pro Lites. But you're not the important guy. We're gonna let you drive, but just stick around, hang out, and we'll get you in there at some point."

I started messing around, just being myself, having fun, and joking around with this older guy who was spraying water on people. I didn't know that he was Clyde Stacy, a billionaire coal-mining magnate, and *he* was the real money behind the series.

I just made a relationship with him, and then I was like, "So hey, where are you guys staying? I want to stay with everyone and have fun and hang out."

They invited me to stay at Robby Gordon's house, so I didn't have to get a hotel room. We had dinner together and then we all went back to the track the next day. I was watching people race all day, and some people were having a hard time, flipping the trucks over.

I approached it like a student, just like I had approached snowboarding, trying to learn from their mistakes. Whenever someone got out of that truck, I was asking them questions: *What's going on? What is it like? What did you learn? What did you do wrong?*

I was trying to absorb everything that I could. Because I was not a truck racer, not yet anyway. I had just totaled a truck, and now I was about to get a chance to drive this badass truck? Amazing.

When I finally got my shot to drive it, I ended up being one of the faster guys, just because I had listened and talked to everybody and learned from their mistakes. I did well and I think it surprised a lot of people. Then we parted ways, and I flew home.

Clyde, the guy who was funding everything, said to me, "Man, we really need a guy like you in this series."

"You're damn straight you do," I replied, with this big childish grin on my face.

So I kept racing Pro Lite trucks, and I stayed in touch with all these people.

———————

Clyde had a master plan, and he made me an amazing offer.

"We need a guy like you in this series, but we need to get your résumé better," Clyde said. "You need to come down to Mexico for the Baja 1000."

The Baja 1000 is one of the most prestigious off-road races in the world.

"Yeah, cool," I said. "That sounds fun."

I thought he meant to watch.

"No," Clyde said. "You're gonna race. We're gonna put you in a truck. And we're gonna make sure that you win this race. And you're gonna be able to put that on your résumé."

"Let's do it," I said. "Awesome!"

They flew me in their private jet to Mexico. They had this big compound down there. We were staying at this house that they rented and they had all these different vehicles—I don't even know how many vehicles they had that year, probably six.

It was just crazy. I was staying with Robby Gordon. I was supposed to go pre-running the next day, which is practicing on the course. You were supposed to be taking notes so that when it was time to race, you knew what to expect. You knew where the bad parts were and you noted them on the GPS.

For some reason, they didn't have enough guys to go pre-run and drive. Clyde was like, "I'm just going to take you with me tomorrow, and you'll make notes on my GPS. And we're going to go out in my pre-runner."

Clyde's pre-runner was a $650,000 race truc—built by the Geiser brothers, the same guys who rebuilt my truck for $100 in Phoenix. Clyde's truck was fully enclosed with windows so the dust couldn't get in. It was basically a badass regular truck, but it might as well have been a race truck. In the morning, we got up, jumped in this truck, went to the gas station, and gassed up. Then, we got back in the vehicle, and I looked over at him and saw him put his lap belt on.

These race trucks had a five-point harness seatbelt system that basically locked you in place. The straps went over your shoulders, around your waist, and up through the crotch, and they all buckled together. With that sucker on, you didn't go anywhere.

But he only put his lap belt on.

"What are you doing?" I asked.

"Oh, we're not racing," he said. "We're just driving down the road, just a few miles to the racecourse. And then we're gonna stop at the racetrack and we're gonna get ready."

"Oh," I said. "OK."

But I decided that I was still gonna buckle up. I didn't put the shoulder straps on, but I fastened the lap belt, along with the crotch belt, and I cinched it down tight like I was going racing.

Heading out, we started driving down the road to go to the racetrack. We were following a chase truck filled with parts and supplies and local guys Clyde had hired. They had so much passion and love for this sport. Clyde did all he could to give back to the community where we raced. He was that kind of a guy. It was such an honor to be part of their team.

———

Then, something wild happened. And it all started because of a blinker.

In Mexico, they turn their left blinker on, and it means you are clear to pass. It also means: *I'm f—in' turning left.*

You can imagine that could set up some problems.

So, this guy in front of us put his blinker on, and our chase truck went flying by. Then Clyde punched it. We were doing 85 miles per hour, and he went to pass the guy.

"Dude, that f—er is turning," I said.

As we passed him, the guy turned left and tagged us in the back fender. We turned sideways on the highway going 85 miles per hour and started rolling. We rolled five times off the road. Just chaos. We came to rest on the truck's side, on my door. Then the chase truck backed up to us. I checked myself. "Holy shit," I said, not seeing any blood. "I'm good. I'm good."

I looked over at Clyde, and he was moaning and bleeding.

"Holy shit," I said.

I unbuckled myself. The chase truck backed up to the hood of the truck, which was facing the road because it was on its side. I unbuckled Clyde. I was passing this billionaire out of the window of this truck. They pulled him out and put him in the back of the chase truck and took off, rushing him to the hospital.

I got out. We had just rolled at 85 miles an hour, five times off the highway. But the truck was built for that. We tipped the truck back over. This guy driving a Volkswagen bug showed up. He was the cousin of one of the guys working for our team, because we had hired local guys to work for us. He jumped in the truck and fired it up and took off, because if the cops had showed up, we assumed they would have impounded the truck. If that happened, it might never come back with any of that stuff in it. People break in and steal crap. It was crazy.

We had to pay off the cops. We had to pay off everyone. We had to go buy the guy that hit us a new truck. Just nuts.

We had to rent a plane to fly in from San Diego because Clyde's plane had left.

By the time Clyde got out of the hospital, it was dark, and in Mexico, you couldn't fly at night because of the cartels. Everything was locked down. So, we had to pay off the airport. A couple of guys and me dragged this billionaire onto this f—ing plane and lay him out on the floor. Then, they took off and flew him to San Diego. Just crazy.

That was my first experience with desert racing.

We actually kept pre-running in that truck that we rolled, broken windows and all. But it still worked fine. I ended up racing in the Baja 1000, an incredible test of endurance and speed on Mexico's Baja California Peninsula. Through rain, heat, dust, and silt, I picked up the truck at the halfway point, drove 510 miles through the night and into the next day, and ended up winning the Baja 1000.

Just so they could put that on my résumé.

Years later, I would think back on that experience. Meeting Clyde. Rolling five times in a truck. Passing a freakin' billionaire through a truck window. The cartels and paying people off. Getting to race on Clyde's team. And it's absolutely wild to me, almost hard to believe. What an amazing opportunity. What a wild time. But it happened because I made it happen. Because I took a chance. Because I was willing to do whatever it took to be able to live the life I wanted. And I just hope kids can learn from that. I hope Landon can follow his dreams and create the life he wants.

Six days before the end of the 2012–13 snowboard season, I was in Spain, and I got a call from off-road racer Justin Matney, one of my good friends.

"Hey, can you be in Arizona in six days?" Matney asked.

Clyde was backing the series, but Matney was one of his partners.

"Yes, I can," I said.

"We're gonna put you in a truck for the season," Matney said.

Heck, yeah!

So, I flew to Arizona to race trucks. I had never raced trucks before, and now I was racing in not one but two professional series.

In the big picture, I figured that it would only help my snowboarding career because it would keep me sharp during the summer. To win on the snowboard, I needed to push the limit, tiptoeing across the thin line that separates danger from safety, which was what I experienced when racing trucks. I was still snowboarding in the winter and then started racing trucks in the summer in stadiums all over the country. Of course, that lead to some crazy crashes. For me, it was all the same thing. It was testing myself, putting myself on that edge of danger, whether it was on the snowboard, on my mountain bike screaming down a trail through the forest, or wide open at 100 miles per hour in a race truck. That only came from pushing the limit. Every chance I got.

April 23, 2013
Long Beach, California
Grand Prix of Long Beach

Sometimes all these trips around the country led to some crazy situations.

We were racing trucks in Long Beach, and Arie Luyendyk Jr., who is a Dutch-American auto racing driver and the son of two-time Indianapolis 500 winner Arie Luyendyk, came up to me and introduced me to a couple women.

"How are you guys doing?" I said. "Great to meet you."

I walked off to do something else.

Later on, Arie couldn't believe it.

"Dude, that girl was into you," he said.

"Yeah, whatever," I said. "Oh, cool. Yeah."

I was trying to focus on the race and doing the best that I could. There would be plenty of time to chase girls later.

The next day, I was out on a run and I got a call from my agent, Carie Goldberg Trutanich. I had met her in 2009 when I went out to stay with my cousin, Natalie Tirapelli, and train at a place called Athletes Performance.

"I'm listening to the radio—*On Air with Ryan Seacrest*," she said. "And they are talking about you. About how Ryan's assistant met a snowboarder yesterday and he's racing trucks. Can you get on the phone with Ryan Seacrest right now?"

"What? Sure," I said, laughing.

She knew someone at the show and called the show and told them, "Hey, you guys are talking about my client."

I stopped running and sat down on the steps.

I talked to Seacrest on the radio, and he proposed setting me up on a date with his assistant.

"Absolutely," I said. I was single. "Love to."

To be honest, at that time, I didn't really know who he was talking about, but as the conversation went on, I realized it was one of the girls with Arie.

"Well, are you paying, Ryan?" I asked.

"Only if you make it to first base," Ryan said.

So, I agreed to go on the date with Tanya Rad, his assistant.

I showed up at the restaurant driving Ben Gulak's DTV Shredder that had tank tracks on it. It was the coolest thing

I'd ever seen, and it was so badass that a cop stopped me and asked, "What is that?"

Talking to the cop, it must have looked like I just got pulled over.

Anyhow, I popped a wheelie pulling up to the restaurant, and I walked in and gave Tanya a hug.

She had long blond hair. I was wearing jeans, a black hoodie, a baseball cap, and a white shirt.

"How are you?" I asked.

"Good, how are you?" she asked.

I shook hands with Nelson Aguirre, an assistant producer from the show. I couldn't quite figure out why she had brought a guy on the date with her.

"Are you trying to keep her safe?" I asked.

A video crew from the Seacrest show taped the entire date and put together a nine-minute video, and it felt like I was on *The Bachelor*, because interviews were intermingled with clips from the date.

"Do you hunt deer?" Nelson asked me.

"I haven't been much of a deer hunter over the years," I said.

"Do you hunt women?" Tanya asked, jumping in.

"Here's what most people would say," I said calmly, grabbing a gyro. "Most guys would say no, I'm not like that and I'm different. And I'm gonna say, I'm a guy. And if there's only one way to meet a girl, and that's if you're walking around and you meet a girl you go talk to her. Most people consider that hunting, I would consider that starting a conversation."

She smiled and Nelson nodded his head.

"He just seems like the kind of guy that's like, no BS," Tanya said in an interview, spliced into that moment on the video. "He just shoots it straight. He's not gonna lie to you. He puts it all on the table, and I admire that."

"How many kids do you want?" she asked.

"Before, I thought I was always gonna have a bunch of kids," I said. "But I have one now. So I'm okay with one, but it's all when I meet that person. I mean, I'm sure we'll hash that out. But I'm totally okay with more as long as my boy is okay with it, Landon."

"Is he as crazy as you are?" Nelson asked.

"No, he's a little more reserved," I said. "Not quite as wild as me. Shy. Just like me. Super shy."

They laughed.

"Maybe he'll come out of his shell," she said.

"Oh, I'm sure he will," I said.

And I believe that.

"Nick seems to be a really great father," she said in an interview. "That's one thing I definitely keyed in on in the middle of our date when he was talking about his son. He was so genuine and sweet, and I think that they have a really great relationship."

Nelson spoke up.

"Do you want me to tell you something?" Nelson said. "I know this is so weird. But in the beginning, I didn't know what to expect. And I think you are a great guy."

"What did you think?" I asked, smiling. "You thought I was gonna be a typical—"

"I thought you were gonna be a douche," he said. "And you are actually a really nice guy. And I think Tanya is also very surprised by this. You know what? You turned out to be very, very interesting."

"I hear that quite a bit because people will naturally just think I'm a typical jock, meathead," I said.

"Yep, correct," she said.

I put on my gruff meathead voice: "What's up...woman!"

"You come off a little like that," she said.

"You do," Nelson said. "But it's OK. It's kind of like a shield for you."

"I think Nick is awesome," Nelson said in an interview on the video. "He talks so highly of his kid and how he's working hard right now, spending a lot of time away from him but he wants to be there with him and when he's there with him at home, he's hanging out with him. He just talked so good about his kid."

The night ended with a hug.

I was single—by choice. Because of Landon.

After Landon was born, Landon's mom and I tried to make it work, even when I went to Colorado. We actually almost got married. But we decided that it was best if we weren't together because we were fighting, and we didn't want to do that in front of Landon. We were young and didn't know what we were doing. I had one girlfriend right after Landon's mother. We dated for two years, and I immediately saw how much time I could have been spending with my son rather than putting that time and effort into a relationship. For me, it was kind of like, *All right, dude, you did this. You made this bed; it's time to lie in it and be there for your son.*

He was the most important thing to me. By not having a relationship with someone in the Upper Peninsula, when I went home I wouldn't have to spend time trying to make a relation-ship work. I could spend that time with my son. When I was gone, rather than calling home and trying to keep my girlfriend happy, I could call and talk to my son and do those kinds of things. For me, it was more of a situation where I thought, *Hey, man, you need to put this time and effort into your son and maybe once he's grown and out of the house, then you can start to maybe work at a relationship becoming a little more serious.*

But that just hadn't happened. My travel schedule was way too grueling, right person or not.

June 8, 2013
St. Louis, Missouri
Stadium Super Truck Races

I freakin' can't believe it. This is wild...so surreal.

Inside the Edward Jones Dome, I stood on a podium with Robby Gordon and Rob MacCachren. I had taken third place in the Stadium Super Truck race in St. Louis, and that meant I was on a podium with two of the biggest names in off-road racing.

Here I was, just this crazy kid from the Upper Peninsula who talked his way into this sport because of snowboarding, talked his way into sponsorships, blindly sent an email and got into this series...standing there with legends.

Holy shit.... Look at this.... Two of the biggest names in the sport, and I'm just this crazy dreamer standing in this company. Pretty amazing.

I was still bopping between worlds—from truck racing to snowboarding and back to truck racing. After finishing a Super Truck race in Los Angeles in the spring of 2013, I jumped on a flight to Mount Hood, a couple of days before our snowboarding training camp.

Lindsey Jacobellis went early, too, because she was coming back from a torn anterior cruciate ligament. She had surgery and lost part of the 2012 season and all of the 2013 season. Lindsey and I went out and rode together so she could see how her knee was feeling.

When an athlete comes back from injury, there are always mental hurdles and questions. I'm sure she had worries—*How will my knee handle this? Will I be as strong? Will I be as fearless?*

So, I knew she was in a tough place mentally, and she wanted to see how her knee would respond. She was nervous and apprehensive. She took a turn and I tried to encourage her. "You are doing it," I said.

She made another turn. "You are turning!" I said.

I was just trying to give her some support, trying to keep her spirits up. We were like family—a brother and sister in snowboarding. We were always in each other's corners. We had spent so much time together. Sometimes it felt like we were siblings and we wanted to scream at each other. But when one of us needed help, we were always there for each other…100 percent invested in each other.

We ripped a few turns and she was smiling and having fun and it seemed like she was saying, *All right, all good; I can do this.*

———————

My life had turned into an nonstop whirlwind. I was truck racing, snowboard training, jumping on planes, checking in and out of hotels, and constantly working to get sponsors. I loved it, chasing all of it—the Olympics, X Games—and I could make money doing it. Not a lot, but I could make money. I was surviving, and it allowed me to travel the world. It was amazing to get the chance to do something at the highest level. Something I loved doing. Most people don't get that opportunity. And I was doing it in multiple sports.

In my mind, to have the chance to race all year long was an incredible advantage because it kept me fresh. To be good at snowboarding, I figured I had to live on that edge—at all times. Flirting with disaster. Being comfortable in the uncomfortable.

Other snowboarders would take the summer off and then have to start cold again on snow.

But I was bouncing off the rev limiter at all times.

GO! GO! GO!

But it also came with a huge cost.

All that traveling took me away from Landon. I was on the road all summer—Landon would come to some races—but I'd have to put so much time and effort and energy in trying to keep everything together, it was weighing on me. Tina was an amazing mother. There was no way I could have done this without her busting ass or without my parents picking up the responsibility when I was on the road.

But I got to a point where I realized, *I can't do this anymore.*

I needed to focus on trying to be a dad.

I gave up truck racing to concentrate on snowboarding.

But mostly, to be a dad.

CHAPTER 9

NEVER HALF-ASS ANYTHING

ON THE BUBBLE ONCE AGAIN.

Heading into the 2014 Winter Olympics, I didn't know if I would make the team.

Two-time Olympian Nate Holland, Trevor Jacob, and Alex Deibold had all locked up spots through automatic qualifying. That left one more open spot, and it was down to me and my friend, two-time gold medalist Seth Wescott. I figured I was in a good position. I was the only American man with three top-10 finishes in World Cup races. Seth was coming back from an injury—a ripped-up knee and a broken tibia—but he had a chance to become the first American male to win a Winter Olympic event three times.

So, at X Games, the coaches gave him one last shot to make the team. If Seth did well and proved that his knee was healthy and he was back to form, then the coaches were going to take him instead of me. That put me in a strange position. I thought I had earned the spot, but I also understood their reasoning. Seth had enjoyed tremendous success at the two previous Olympics. So, I had to respect the decision.

At X Games, Seth took fifth in his quarterfinal heat. He was done for the day. One thing I'll never forget—on the ESPN broadcast, Seth said that he hoped that I would do well in my race. He wasn't rooting for me to fail. I had to respect him for that.

In my quarterfinal, another rider crashed into me, and I also finished in fifth place.

So, what the heck were the coaches going to do?

If I didn't make it, it was nobody's fault but my own. I had put myself in this situation.

But I still felt good. My riding was as strong as it had ever been. And I fully believed that if I was picked, I would medal at the Olympics.

We went into the athletes' lounge, where the coaches were standing around. They looked at me and said, "Baum, we're picking you for the Olympics."

I was relieved and thrilled, excited and thankful. Just so happy.

"Can I tell my parents and can they tell people?" I asked.

"Absolutely."

My first call was to Stambaugh Elementary. Landon, who was nine at the time, was in the fourth grade. They patched me through to his classroom and I made the announcement to his class.

But mostly to my son.

"Landon, I'm going back to the Olympics," I said.

I could barely get the words out without choking up.

Landon and his classmates started screaming.

"Good luck!" they screamed.

It was unbelievable.

Nick playing T-ball with the older boys.
Credit: Nick Baumgartner

With older brother Rob on a fishing trip and came across a snapping turtle. Rob taught Nick all about the outdoors.
Credit: Nick Baumgartner

Nick (third from left) and his three older brothers.
Credit: Nick Baumgartner

Nick and his sister, Ida, for their fall sports picture in 1999 at West Iron County High School where Nick was a multi-position football player and Ida was a cheerleader.
Credit: Nick Baumgartner

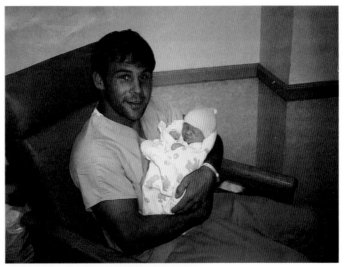

First time holding Landon right after he was born.
Credit: Nick Baumgartner

Nick's sister, Ida; dad, Bob; and mom, Mary, road-tripped it from Iron River, Michigan, to Aspen, Colorado, together for Nick's first Winter X Games in 2005.
Credit: Nick Baumgartner

2011 X Games gold medal win holding six-year-old Landon at his first race watching Dad.
Credit: Rustin Gudim/ZUMAPRESS/Newscom

Nick with Shaun Palmer, former U.S. Snowboard teammate, goofing around wearing a USA Wrestling singlet while Shaun wears Lederhosen. Palmer is considered one of the forefathers of extreme sports and was Nick's biggest influence to start racing snowboard cross. Teammate Graham Watanabe is laughing in the background.
Credit: Nick Baumgartner

Nick stamping concrete at a friend's home in Iron River.
Credit: Nick Baumgartner

Proud Baumgartner family moment after Nick won gold at the 2011 Winter X Games with his dad, Bob; mom, Mary; and son, Landon.
Credit: Paul Henderson

2013 Stadium Super Trucks race in St. Louis. Nick takes third alongside off-road racing legends Rob MacCachren and Robby Gordon.
Credit: Kevin Wilson

Nick's 2014 U.S. Olympic headshot.
Credit: Getty Images

2014 Summer X Games racing in a Stadium Super Truck on the F1 Track in Austin, Texas.
Credit: Dan Wozniak/ZUMA Press/Newscom

2017 World Championship gold medal team win with Hagen Kearney in Sierra Nevada, Spain.
Credit: Getty Images

2018 PyeongChang Winter Olympics send-off pep rally with son Landon at West Iron County High School/Charles Greenlund Gymnasium.
Credit: Nick Baumgartner

2018 PyeongChang Winter Olympics. Nick went to the *TODAY Show* set to meet Savannah Guthrie and Hoda Kotb.
Credit: Nick Baumgartner

2018 Athlete Processing in Munich, Germany, getting outfitted in the U.S. Olympic Opening Ceremony gear.
Credit: Nick Baumgartner

2018 PyeongChang Winter Olympics after Nick's semifinal run.
Credit: Getty Images

2018 PyeongChang Winter Olympics Closing Ceremony carrying U.S. skiing legend Lindsey Vonn.
Credit: Nick Baumgartner

Crossing the finish line first in the 2022 Winter Olympics mixed-team final.
Credit: Getty Images

Embracing U.S. teammate Lindsey Jacobellis after winning the gold medal in mixed-team competition.
Credit: Getty Images

Showing elation upon Lindsey Jacobellis crossing the finish line in first place, securing the gold medal for them in the mixed-team event.
Credit: Getty Images

2022 Beijing Winter Olympics medal ceremony with Lindsey Jacobellis.
Credit: Getty Images

2022 Welcome Home Parade.
Nick walking along the streets of Iron River, Michigan, with his dog, Oakley, leading the way and high-fiving Gary Richards of Ski Brule.
Credit: Kevin Zini

2022 Welcome Home Parade with Nick giving high-fives to the kids with his dog, Oakley, by his side.
Credit: Krist Oil

2022 Welcome Home Parade coming down Genesee Street in Iron River, Michigan.
Credit: Kevin Zini

2022 Welcome Home Parade ending at West Iron County High School surrounded by friends and family.
Credit: Kevin Zini

2022 NFL Thanksgiving game between the Detroit Lions and Buffalo Bills. Nick was an honored guest.
Credit: Detroit Lions

Nick doing the Lambeau Leap at the Green Bay Packers' game against the L.A. Rams on December 19, 2022.
Credit: Getty Images

February 2014
Sochi, Russia
2014 Winter Olympics

I'm a Yooper. I like to have fun. I'm happy. I'm smiley. I talk to everybody, even when they don't understand me.

When I first started snowboarding, a couple of teams didn't know any English—like the guys on the Japanese team, for instance. But I was always playing charades, trying to communicate with them through exaggerated hand gestures—the only way I knew.

I tried to talk to the Russians without speaking Russian. I was acting crazy, being myself. And it got to the point where they would just see me coming and start laughing. I didn't know if they were laughing at me or with me, but I was getting smiles out of people. So I liked it.

It was just my little piece of international diplomacy.

I didn't go to Russia to take second or third. I went there to win. But the setup was less than ideal. We took one look at the course and a long list of athletes and coaches—snowboarders and skiers—blasted Sochi's courses, in the media and behind the scenes.

Australian women's halfpipe favorite Torah Bright, who crashed in training, said the people who constructed the course "aren't the greatest at their craft."

Shaun White, perhaps the biggest U.S. star, said the course was "far from perfect."

In the women's slopestyle freestyle skiing heats, gold medal favorite Kaya Turski—the world champion—crashed on both her runs. In the moguls, there were numerous crashes, and Heidi Kloser, an American, tore up her knee and broke a thigh bone in another accident.

The course was big and fun but the weather made it a mess. When reporters asked me about the conditions, I tried to put a good spin on it. "If it's dangerous and scary and I can overcome it and do well—I'm looking for that rush, that adrenaline," I told reporters. "It's the reason I do it. It's what brought me to the sport."

But it wasn't just the course. The weather was horrible in Sochi.

I compete in an outdoor sport. Bad weather—on both extremes, too hot or too cold—is always part of the equation. It's going to happen.

But in Russia, the weather felt like a spring day—or maybe a June day in the Upper Peninsula. Rainy. Warm temperatures. Melting snow. A sloppy, slushy mess. Just gnarly weather conditions for snowboarding. The day we were supposed to qualify, it was so foggy that you couldn't even see your hand in front of your face, so they ended up canceling the event.

When we raced the next day, in far from ideal conditions, we faced pouring rain for training, which was fine. We had waxed for those conditions. We were waiting but they didn't do a time trial. They just seeded us by our world ranking, which put me in the first heat. They had a bunch of younger kids, younger Russian athletes, testing the course with us. They were the forerunners. All week, the forerunners kept getting hurt on and hauled off the big, dangerous track.

About 15 minutes before the first heat dropped, it started to snow from turn one to the top of the mountain. It got really snowy up above, and then below turn one, it was still raining.

They didn't have a forerunner go out of the gate that I went on.

Looking back, we should have said something—myself or one my coaches. That was super unfair and not ideal for the biggest event in the world.

———————

I pulled out of the gate and my snowboard went nowhere. By the first turn I was so far behind everybody. We got to turn one and my snowboard took off again and I caught back up to everyone and had to make an aggressive move in the second-to-last corner. It was a move that didn't pay off, and I took fourth out of five.

I didn't advance through that first round and I was thinking, *This can't be happening. Not here.*

I spent the rest of the first round standing in the finish area, completely dejected, shaking my head in disgust, staring at the large video screen, watching the rest of the competition.

"I didn't really get going and the rhythm never started," I told reporters. "What are you going to do? Today was a bad day to have a bad day, though. My timing was off and I was doing great in the training days. [The rain] doesn't help. It slows things down, just makes things a little bit different and I didn't adjust well."

I was dying inside.

"Ten years trying for an Olympic medal, to have it over that quick, it's a tearjerker," I told a reporter. "But what are you going to do? Use it as fire or let it take you down? I'm going to use it as fire and come back in Korea [in 2018] hopefully and give it another shot."

———————

Then, things went from bad to worse. The internet went crazy and I started to get bashed:

Why did we take this guy instead of a two-time gold medalist?
This guy sucks.
He has no business representing us.

I saw some of the posts, and it hurt. I was getting torn apart. I think sometimes people forget that we're just human beings out there. I had friends who would contact me: "Did you see what so-and-so wrote about you?"

Yeah, um, gee thanks for pointing that out.

The criticism kept getting worse:

What a waste!

Why did we take this guy?

He should have never been there.

Why would we waste our time bringing this guy to the Olympics?

I could have let them hurt my feelings. Could have let them break me down. Could have quit. I could have said all right, you know what, this is too hard. I can't do this. But man, I loved it. It became motivation. I turned it into fuel.

OK. Wait until you see what happens in 2018. I'm gonna win a medal and I'm gonna show you with my actions, instead of my words.

I just wanted it so bad. And I wanted to get that Olympic gold medal.

It was so important to keep fighting for it.

———————

Years later, when I reflected on what went wrong, I had to be honest with myself. Heading into the 2014 Olympics, I slacked off. I didn't work as hard as I should have. I definitely cut corners. I had spent too much time in the offseason racing trucks and chasing the rush rather than in a gym preparing for the season. I thought I was helping myself in the trucks—and that's what I told myself—but maybe it was the opposite. Maybe I was hurting my snowboarding career.

In Russia, yes, the weather was horrible. It screwed me in my eyes. But I could have worked way harder for that Olympics. I could have done a lot more. It was a wasted opportunity, and I blame only myself.

I started to come to a conclusion: *You can never half-ass anything. If you do everything in your power and don't cut any corners and then you fall short, you can live with that. But when you cut corners and fall short, it will haunt you for the rest of your life.*

CHAPTER 10

THE DAY I FELT OLD

December 17, 2017
Montafon, Austria

People ask me, "When did you start to feel old?"

I know exactly when it happened.

It was at noon Austria time on my 36th birthday. We were in the first heat of a team race. I was partnered with Mick Dierdorff, a great friend who would become a two-time Olympian and the 2019 World Champion.

At that time, two men were paired together in the team races.

I was battling against Lorenzo Sommariva, an Italian, through the first corner. He reached out and started grabbing me with his front arm. I swung my arm to break his grip, and as we were racing through the roller pack, one the cameras picked up my audio perfectly.

"Dude, what the f—k!"

Entering turn two, I slipped into the lead. Coming out of the turn, I got too aggressive on a jump. I came up a little short and lost speed. That allowed Lorenzo to dive to the inside of the next corner. Rather than hold his line, he crossed into my lane and took out the nose of my board as we went off a jump.

The idiot. It took both of us out.

I crashed hard, the worst I had ever experienced, and the wind was knocked out of me.

Gasping for air, struggling to breathe, it felt like someone had just hit me in the middle of my spine with a sledgehammer.

The ski patrol came up to me: "Are you OK? Are you OK?"

But I couldn't answer.

I couldn't breathe or talk.

It seemed as if minutes had passed, even though I knew it was probably much less than that.

As soon as I got my breath and could mumble some words, I yelled, "Did that f—er wipe out, too?"

I was so angry. He had made a stupid and dangerous move, putting both of us at risk.

Ski patrol was pretty sure that I had broken my back, and I was strapped to a board.

The pain was excruciating. I was complaining and screaming as they hooked up an IV.

"Give him some more fentanyl!" Dierdorff demanded.

When the pain started to get manageable, I called my mom. I was crying, not sure what this meant, but I knew it was bad.

"They are going to take me in a helicopter to the hospital," I told my mom.

The same helicopter that took me to the hospital a few years earlier when I was knocked out cold in a training run.

"Tell Landon I love him," I told my mom. I was really dramatic, like those were my last words and I was going down in an airplane crash.

Everyone started crying.

"Dude, this is not good," I said to Dierdorff. "This could be it."

I feared my snowboard career could be over.

They didn't let me sit up. Heck, they didn't let me move, waiting for the helicopter.

Eventually, they loaded me into a bird and flew me off the mountain. I was afraid any movement, or any jolt from the helicopter, was going to leave me paralyzed.

X-rays revealed that I had compressed three vertebrae in my mid-back (T9, T11, and T12). The doctor explained it to me and all I heard, or remembered, was that my body basically folded in half like a suitcase.

Finally, after all the imaging was done, I was allowed to sit up, which was terrifying. I was still afraid of being paralyzed.

"Can I still compete?" I asked.

It was an Olympic year and I had a shot to make the team.

"You can't hurt it any worse than it is," the doctor assured me. "It will be painful, but you're not going to cause any more damage. If you can handle the pain, you can race."

I tried to walk around, and the pain was tremendous.

"This hurts, but I might be able to do this," I said.

I got up and started walking around the room a little bit, and the competitor in me kicked in. It didn't matter how much it might hurt. I saw possibility.

"Holy shit, dude, we got a shot," I said. "We got another race in three days in Italy, and I'm gonna try for it."

The next day I piled into the front seat of the van, and Seth Wescott drove us from Austria six hours across Switzerland into Italy to Cervinia. It was, by far, the most painful ride of my life. When we stopped for gas, I got out and did a little test jump to see if it hurt when I landed. The pain was excruciating.

I skipped training to get one more day of rest. I went up for the qualifying day, took one training run, and was crying in pain at the bottom.

"I can't do this," I said.

I was bawling.

"Listen, man, I can't do it," I said to my coach, Peter Foley.

"Hey, it's okay," Foley said. "This isn't the end. We don't know what this means."

"But what about the Olympics?" I asked.

"This doesn't mean you are not going," he said.

"Yeah, but this means I'm not competing in the Olympic qualifier," I said. "So, it's not good."

I walked off and they started the first round of racing. I waited until it was my spot, and I decided not to race.

"Okay, now I can go back," I said. "I missed my spot, I'm done."

There were two chances to qualify, and I had just missed the first one. I grabbed all my stuff and headed down to the hotel. I reached a point where I could turn left and go to the hotel…or I could turn right and go back to the chairlift and go back up.

I stopped and turned right.

"Ah, f—k it; we're doing it," I said.

I got back up to the top and saw my coach.

"What are you doing?" Foley asked.

"I'm gonna go ask them," I said. "If they say I can race, I'm gonna try."

"All right," he said. "Whatever you think."

They let me race.

I was timid and cautious, finishing a half-second off qualifying. For good reason. Had I raced hard and aggressive, I probably would have hurt myself even more. Some people did get hurt during that race. So it turned into a good thing that I couldn't do it.

The next day, I sat at the hotel and watched my teammate, Alex Deibold, make it to the finals. He ended up fourth, setting himself up for one of the Olympic spots, and I thought, *I'm in real trouble. I really have to crush it at the next race in Turkey just to make the Olympics.*

I went home to Iron River and took about a month off to rest.

Four weeks later, we flew to Turkey and I finished in fourth place, qualifying for the Olympics.

February 2018
PyeongChang, South Korea
2018 Winter Olympics

About six weeks after crashing in Austria, getting ready to compete in my third Olympics, my body was still beat up. I was still recovering from three crushed vertebrae, a broken rib, and two bruised lungs. But I was stoked to have another shot.

"I'm feeling better than ever," I told reporters.

OK, that was a *little* lie. I was still recovering from a broken back.

"I wasn't going to let that get in the way of this," I told them. "Sometimes you just have to bite down and go."

Reporters kept asking me questions:

How can you do it with those injuries?

How do you deal with the pain?

How will it hurt you in competition?

In my eyes, it all went back to my training and preparation. If you make your body strong enough, you can handle anything. And there was one other thing. A huge thing, really—Landon was coming to his first Olympics. There was no way I was going to let this stop me.

———————

The course was dangerous and had a lot of problems.

"You gotta change this," I told the coursebuilders and the organizer. "You gotta fix the jumps."

All the riders spoke up and shared our concerns, but the organizers thought they knew better than we did.

For the first two days of training, I kept asking them to fix the issues.

After the third and final day of training, I firmly said, "If you don't change it, you are going to f—ing kill someone."

But the organizer thought he knew better than us.

Then, Markus Schairer, an Austrian, broke his neck. We were going full speed into this straightaway. There was a G force when you hit the lip of the jump, and we were jumping super high—maybe 20 or 30 feet in the air. Markus started rotating and landed gruesomely on his neck and upper back, fracturing his fifth cervical vertebra.

"You f—ing need to listen to us!" I said.

Nine people would end their season on this Olympic course, three of them ending their careers because of injuries.

That was just on the men's side. But on the women's side, it was the same thing. There were women in freakin' wheelchairs and crutches getting onto the bus.

In the semifinals, I took a jump, overshot the landing, and crashed. But I got up and finished the race. That turned into a lucky break, because other racers crashed behind me and only one rider had passed me. I finished in second and advanced to the final.

I stood at the bottom of the hill and screamed, "Yeah! Landon!"

Then, I directed a TV cameraman to take Landon's picture.

"Somebody upstairs loves me!" I screamed.

Unfortunately, in the final, I didn't have my best start

Mick Dierdorff, Alex "Chumpy" Pullin, and I were alongside each other about halfway down the track. We were directly behind Regino Hernandez, Pierre Vaultier, and Jarryd Hughes. The draft from those guys pulled us and threw us into the air—soaring off the jump that claimed most of the injured riders.

We were screaming and cursing, knowing that we were about to fall from the sky. If we were mic'd up, it would have sounded like we were going down in a plane crash.

I used all of my suspension and crumbled to the ground, trying to absorb the impact the best I could. I shot back to my feet, getting up the fastest, and continued.

I finished in fourth. France's Vaultier won his second straight gold medal in the event, Australia's Hughes earned silver, and Spain's Hernandez took bronze.

After swallowing some of the pain, I stood up and looked for Landon. He was beaming with pride. I could see it in his face, and it was the most amazing feeling.

If he wasn't disappointed at all, how could I be?

I limped through the snow, my left heel badly bruised from the vicious, painful landing.

"Yeah, Yoopers do it big!" I screamed while talking to a TV reporter. "But it's cool. It's the biggest event. I'm 36 years old. To be here, representing the U.S., my hometown in the U.P., my family—man, I'm on top of the world."

I took off my bib and put it on Landon, hoping that would allow him to go through security and enter the mixed zone with the reporters. Yeah, I was probably breaking all kinds of rules. But I didn't care. I wanted him to experience this with me. With his old man. To see all of this through my eyes. I wanted him to get a taste of what it was like to be an Olympian.

"Fourth place!" I said to Landon in front of the reporters. "The wooden spoon. Just think how famous you would be at school if I was on the podium."

Landon smiled—he couldn't stop smiling. This was my third Olympics, but the first time that he'd watched me in person.

"I think he's pretty awesome," Landon told reporters.

"That's a heck of a quote to hear as a dad," I said.

I smiled, the pain throbbing through my foot from the crash.

"Unbelievable!" I said. "As a parent, to still be competing at 36 years old, to have my son here, to show him with my actions that you can do anything you want to do. Dream big! Unbelievable!"

"What is next?" a reporter asked. "How long can you keep doing this?"

"If [Tom] Brady can do it, Baumgartner can do it," I said. "I'll be here in four years—absolutely! I'm still hunting for one of those medals. This is my third Games. If I gotta go until I'm 100 to get a medal, I'm going to keep doing it."

It was more than a quote.

It was a vow. Not just to the world. But to myself.

We finished the interviews and the crowd started to disappear. The TV cameras were being packed up and reporters were walking back to a building at the base of the mountain to write their stories.

I tried to walk through the snow, but I couldn't put any weight on my foot. I turned to Landon.

"I'm gonna use you as a crutch," I said, wrapping my arm around my 13-year-old son. I was limping badly, leaning on Landon, as we made our way down a tricky, slippery, snow-covered hill.

Long after the competition, after the interviews were done, after all the TV cameras were gone, I walked across the snow with my son.

We were alone now. Still arm in arm. Making our way. It was such an amazing moment, powerful and profound.

He was holding me up.

Helping me.

A teenager propping up his father.

More than anything, I hoped Landon learned something about perseverance that day. There are going to be times when things are hard, when your body hurts, when nothing comes easy. But it's for a reason. When things don't go your way, that's when you learn. And that's when you can prepare yourself for the greatness to come.

During the closing ceremonies, I was walking with my snowboardcross teammates and freestyler Shaun White, enjoying the moment and taking it all in. I turned around to look at the other Team USA athletes. A little ways back, I saw Lindsey Vonn, one of the best skiers of all time.

"Hey, come on, jump on," I said, pointing to my shoulders. She jumped on my shoulders, and it was funny because our friends didn't know what was going on. My friends were like, "I cannot believe Lindsey Vonn is on your shoulders; what is going on?" Then all her friends were like, "I can't believe Lindsey is on this guy's shoulders."

No one knew that we knew each other. We were both Midwest people. And we became friends in 2010 during processing. She's good people. And yeah, it was cool.

But it was actually turning into our tradition. I actually carried her out in 2010 after my terrible performance, but no one captured it in a photograph. I do remember telling her that I knew how to get publicity back in 2010. I could fall and I kind of shook a little trying to scare her but more trying to be funny.

But here, in 2018, a photographer snapped a picture of us and it went around the world.

This time, we made *USA Today*. Unfortunately for me, the photographer didn't know who I was. The cutline with the picture read, "Fellow U.S. Olympic athlete carries Vonn on his shoulders."

When people looked at that photo, few knew that I was carrying her with a broken back and badly bruised heel.

But I was loving every second of it, enjoying everything about the Olympics.

———————

After the 2018 Olympics, there was a lot of talk about safety. Well, my sport is not safe. And that's why we do it. We understand the risks every time we step out there. And we don't want it to be safe and easy. We're snowboarders; we thrive in that environment. And we love that about our sport. I hope they don't try to make it any softer.

But there is a difference between safe and dangerous.

That 2018 course was dangerous, and they could have fixed it. But they didn't. And several people got hurt because of it.

———————

"Where are you going next?" people around Iron River would ask me. "When are you leaving?"

I had to sheepishly respond, "I really don't know."

Snowboarding had taken me to 20 countries around the world. But I didn't always know where I was heading next.

When I first started racing professionally, I used to get an email telling me when we were traveling. But I got the United app on my phone, and I would check all my upcoming travel on there.

Sometimes I'd meet up with one or two teammates in Chicago or Newark or Washington and we'd fly out together. But usually, we didn't meet up until we got to Zurich, or Frankfurt, or somewhere in Europe.

It was all a blur to me.

Geography-wise, sometimes I had no idea where I was.

"Well, where are you going in Germany?" somebody would ask me.

"I really don't know," I replied. "We are flying to Munich, and then we are driving three hours from there."

"Which direction?"

I had to laugh. "Well, I don't know."

When I first started competing on the U.S. Snowboard Team, the entire team piled into one or two vans, loaded all our board bags on top, and ran ratchet straps over them. And it was kind of a shitshow.

There would be three or four bench seats, and we'd travel all over like that, like some traveling band of snowboard gypsies.

But everything started to change. The snowboarders started traveling in multiple cars and the wax technicians drove a big cargo van that we loaded all our gear into. The cars were a lot more comfortable. We got our own space and it helped keep everyone a lot more cordial. Helped us keep our heads in a good space and focused on the task at hand—winning.

"You get to travel all around the world," people said to me. "You are so lucky."

But I had to laugh. The travel was brutal. I had to lug around two snowboard bags, each one weighing 70 pounds. I also carried a duffel bag that weighed 70 pounds plus a backpack, and sometimes a little wheelie bag.

I was competing in a highly dangerous sport full of crashes and unpredictability. But I always thought the airport was one of the most likely places to get hurt because we had to drag all these huge bags all over the world, lifting them onto vans.

Most of the time in Europe, we stayed in tiny little hotel rooms. It's not like in America where you get two queen beds in a room. In Europe, you get two little tiny beds, probably equivalent to a twin mattress. Two of the beds were always touching, and they shared a headboard. At least they had separate sheets.

U.S. Snowboard has always had, by far, the biggest team. It grew to 17 people, so it became kind of tricky for our coaches to get accommodations for all of us and to try to work out the logistics of everything.

When I first started professionally snowboarding, I left for two weeks, then I went home for a week, and then I'd be gone for two more weeks.

But everything changed.

More events were added in Europe, and that forced us to be gone longer. I'd be gone for a month, go home for two weeks at Christmas, and then go back on the road for a month. We used to skip World Cup races to do sweet pro events in the U.S.—events that paid more money and were aired on U.S. TV. The World Cups, not held in the U.S., were never aired back home.

Luckily, they were broadcast on the CBC, a Canadian channel available in Michigan. So Landon could at least watch me on TV in the U.P.

Every year, it was always different—but the trips got longer. Living out of a suitcase and staying in a tiny little hotel room, crammed together with a roommate…it got old fast.

When you get a hotel room in Europe, it's usually a family-run thing, and you get your room and typically your breakfast and your dinner covered with the price of your stay.

People imagine that we were fed like these racehorses, with everything we needed, always getting the right nutrition, everything to get the best results.

But that was never the case. It was whatever the hotel provided.

Breakfast in Europe wasn't like breakfast in America. In Europe, maybe you would get hard-boiled eggs, but it was usually bread, salami, and cheese. It's nothing like breakfast in the U.P. I never had a good-luck meal. Because I never knew what I would eat. I would just try to eat enough to make sure I wasn't hungry later in the day.

So, we'd eat breakfast together. Find somewhere locally to eat lunch. And then we would all eat at the hotel restaurant again for dinner—usually buffet style. It was not the highest-quality foods—lots of carbs, lots of potatoes and pasta over and over and over again.

Most of the time, I gained at least 10 to 15 pounds every season, just because we weren't eating healthy.

The men's and women's teams traveled together. Obviously, we didn't room together, so we were separated. With the introduction of SafeSport, a program established to prevent abuse of minors and athletes in U.S. Olympic sports, in 2017, it became a lot trickier and more expensive to travel together. We had all these different rules we had to follow. Back in the day, when I started, it was whatever we could afford on our budget. It was kind of loose; we all ran around and did whatever. Every once in a while, we went somewhere and everyone stayed in a condo. But after all the rules were implemented, it became a lot more strict—probably for the better.

Whenever I was in another city, I wore my USA stuff. I was so proud to wear the Red, White, and Blue. To represent our country. I was proud of all the hard work and how it had paid off. I rocked my shit all the time. And I was so thankful to have the freedom to wear it. So many troops fought for those freedoms, fought for those colors. And when you travelled to all these different countries, you appreciated it even more.

We went to some amazing places. Like Spain, which was more of a party area. We'd fly into Malaga, get off the plane, drive straight to the beach, eat lunch, and hang out, walking around. There were nude spots on the beach where people were just laying with their tops off. The locals were just like, *We don't give a shit.... This is where we live.... We're gonna do what we want.*

We would spend a couple hours at the beach and then we'd get in the cars again and drive straight up to the mountain.

Kind of a crazy life.

PART III

CHAPTER 11

LIVING OUT OF A VAN

W E HAD TO GET OUT.

In March 2020, we were in Switzerland at our final race of the year, and there was a huge COVID-19 breakout, just as it was turning into a worldwide pandemic.

There was confusion about the virus. President Donald Trump held a press conference, and he made some vague statements. It sounded like he was going to shut down the U.S. border, preventing anybody from getting in or out.

We didn't want to get trapped in Europe, so we decided to get out. Around three in the morning, Alex Deibold, my roommate, woke me up: "Baum, you have to get up! Wake up!" Making it sound all dramatic, really messing with me. I thought somebody died or something. We packed up and actually stayed the night in the airport hotel. We flew out the next day and got out of town.

I went home to Iron River and went into isolation. I would have lost my damn mind without Oakley, my 10-year-old black lab/pitbull mix rescue dog from the local pound. I was doing workouts in the house, and she was my training partner, keeping me company, jumping on me, crawling underneath me, or licking my face when I was doing planks or push-ups.

Just an amazing dog.

But I was basically stuck. I couldn't make a living because I couldn't pour concrete in Michigan at that time of year. The ground was still frozen. Money was always in the back of my mind. I needed sponsorships. But they were hard to find in the Upper Peninsula, because there is little industry. Most of all, I needed to work just to pay the bills.

I didn't know what I was going to do, until I got a call from Jeremy Johnson, one of my best friends.

"Come down to St. Louis," he said.

"Do you have work?"

"Yeah," he said. "I need help."

"I got nothing going on here," I said. "I'm just in isolation."

"We can be isolated together," he said. "Just go to job sites and come home."

Sold. I packed my tools, put Oakley in my SUV, and headed to St. Louis to help him build some pools. Landon stayed with his mom because she wasn't sure yet how everything would work out with the pandemic. I went down for a month and then returned to Iron River, scooped up Landon, and went out West to work for my brother. Then I went back to St. Louis for two more months.

I was crisscrossing the country, going from one job to the next, doing anything I could to make money and get through the first year of the pandemic.

I was at a crossroads.

I was experiencing a podium drought. I wasn't coming off a good season—no podiums again in 2021—and I figured I had to do something different.

Then everything changed when Dustin Brancheau popped into my life. He owned Advantedge Sports, a training center in Marquette, about one and a half hours away from Iron River.

"Hey, I think we can really help you in your training efforts," Brancheau said.

I felt an instant connection with Brancheau. He played football at Northern Michigan and was a two-time captain. We spoke the same language, and I understood football players. Better yet, he understood football players—err, former football players.

"Awesome," I said. "I'm gonna come up there."

I visited him in Marquette and toured his facility.

"This isn't like training in South Beach, where you go on the beach, and then come work out and then go to nightclubs," Dustin told me.

I didn't want that either.

"There's none of that stuff here," Brancheau said. "You simply come here to work and go back home to sleep, and then repeat that over and over again."

It sounded perfect to me. More than anything, I needed to change how I was training. Just lifting weights wasn't the answer. Racing trucks wasn't the answer. Wakeboarding wasn't the answer. I was getting older and needed to train more efficiently. I couldn't waste my energy or my time. And I was impressed by Brancheau's training program and plan. I needed someone there to hold me accountable and push me, and Dustin was definitely the right guy for that.

In my small corner of the U.P., we didn't have any sports-specific training facilities. I didn't want to just go through motions and destroy my body, like I had done in the past, wondering if it was going to work.

"Come up as many times a week as you can," he said.

I figured out that I could get up to Marquette four days a week to bust some ass, but I had to keep working and saving money to fund my season as well.

I had to decide if I wanted to give myself the best shot at making the Olympics and not live with any regrets.

So I picked the only option that I know: *Go for it, man.*

––––––––––––

Marquette was perfect for me in so many other ways.

I needed to be in a place where I could cross-train, spend time in a gym, go mountain biking, and then turn around and do some swimming in the cold healing waters of Lake Superior. I knew the trails in Marquette were phenomenal. I also wanted to spend a lot of time swimming because it's low-impact training, a great workout without putting strain on my body. For me, just being outside, riding a bike or going swimming, was rejuvenating. I was constantly moving, so everything that I did, I considered training. That's how I approached it.

Even when I was having fun.

There is only one way to stay competitive in a sport for 17 years, and that's to do it for the love of it, not just the competition. At the 2018 Olympics, they dubbed me and my teammates as the last of the blue-collar Olympians, the last of the people who had to fight for it, who had to work for it. These new kids coming in—nothing against them—but they just came from a different place. They had funding. They had resources. They were getting sent to academies when they were young.

But I don't know if they ever learned how to enjoy snowboarding.

Sometimes I would show up at a race venue a few days before a race, and it would dump all kinds of snow. All this deeper powder.

I would see all these other teams on their race boards and their race pants just carving the groomers.

I was like, *What is wrong with you guys? Just enjoy this!*

My team would get our freeride boards out for fun. We'd get out there. Enjoying it. Making turns for fun. And it kept that spirit and fire alive.

If all I did was compete—compete, compete—I would have burned out fast.

I approached my offseason training the same way. I never spent all my time in the gym. I spent time on my mountain bike. I went swimming with Oakley. I paddleboarded with Landon. I canoed and kayaked. I did anything that I could to be outdoors, to keep healthy and fit.

———————

To be able to train and work out all summer without having to pour concrete at the same time, I had to come up with a plan. I went out west and worked with my brother Josh in May. I made a lot more money and did it without any stress. I actually did a big project for David and Renie Gorsuch's store in the Vail Village. David and Renie were both Team USA alpine skiers in the 1960 Olympics, and David was one of Vail's founding fathers. I worked my butt off for a month and made enough money to float me through the summer training block.

The second phase of my work plan was just as important: in the fall, when I knew that money would be short and Landon would be back at school, I would go back out to Colorado and make enough money to be able to pay the bills and cover Landon through the Olympics.

The time in between? That's when I would devote all my time training for the Olympics.

At least, that was the plan.

———————

When I got back from Aspen, I started the most important stretch of training in my life.

Every Monday around 10 AM in the Central Time Zone, I packed up my van and drove one and a half hours to Marquette, which was in the Eastern Time Zone. I'd lose an hour in the drive because of the time change.

I pulled into AdvantEdge Sports and did a workout. The training center was a haven for elite athletes. Brancheau had trained more than 25 professional athletes and 520 college athletes, mostly from Northern Michigan. Some professional boxers and NFL guys trained there during their offseasons because it was so far away from distractions and, like me, they believed in what Dustin was doing.

The big thing was just having someone there holding me accountable. But it was also good not to have to think about my program. I put all my trust in him and let him figure out the plan. Then, I just did it.

Every part of the plan was smart and measured out. Dustin had this device that read the speed of the bar as I was pushing it. So, even if I was tired one day, I was not just in there meathead training, like I had always done in the past, doing bench presses or squats, trying to lift heavy weights just to lift heavy weights. That was the type of weightlifting program I grew up on. The meathead football player plan.

But under Dustin's plan, I was more efficient with my movements, using high tech equipment that measured effort and production.

Almost immediately, I started to see results. Like with my vertical jump—a sign that I was becoming more explosive. I was always able to dunk a women's basketball. The only reason I couldn't dunk a men's basketball was because I couldn't palm it. I was six feet tall, and for most of my career I weighed between 205 and 215 pounds—depending on how many all-you-can-eat buffets I had been to in Europe.

But I never had a good vertical jump because I never trained for it. I never worked on being explosive.

At regular intervals, Dustin tested my vertical jump with pressure plates. Before training, my vertical jump was just 22 inches. Maybe 23. I was never good at that. Not even when I went to play college football. But after some training, it increased by seven inches, which was amazing to me.

I was getting more explosive. At my age—a clear indication this training was working.

So, I kept doing it, going back and forth to Marquette twice a week.

———————

How did a professional snowboarder train during the summer with no snow?

Obviously I didn't live near a glacier, and I couldn't snowboard all year round.

But mountain biking was always my secret training method.

First of all, it was just fun. The trails in Marquette are world class, as good as anything I've ever ridden anywhere.

After working out at AdvantEdge Sports, I left the gym and went riding for two to three hours on the trails around Marquette. Obviously, it helped my leg strength and cardio. But it was more than that. Racing down a winding path on a mountain bike helped train my mind for snowboarding. When you're racing on a snowboard, you have to stay on the edge, hanging between danger and safety. Right on the sweet spot. During the offseason, if you can dip into that sweet spot as much as possible, you start training your mind to be comfortable in the most uncomfortable, hair-raising, white-knuckle moments.

Even though it might sound odd, mountain biking also trained my eyes.

I tried to ride as fast as possible, screaming down the trails. The farther I looked ahead, the faster I went. I was training my peripheral vision to read the terrain on both sides, keeping my mind on edge. It would drive some people crazy. When I went riding with my friends, I got as close to them as possible, to get used to people being around me, working in a crowd, creating a chaotic moment—putting myself in an uncomfortable situation.

Just like in a snowboard race.

Everywhere I went, I took Oakley along.

She was my best friend and my training partner. When I used to do a lot of running—putting in serious miles—we ran together. We did 13 miles around the lake and stopped at a few spots so she could jump in and cool off.

So, of course, she traveled with me to Marquette. When I was in the gym and it was really busy, she stayed outside. I parked next to the open garage door at the gym, so Oakley was right there with me at all times. She would just lay there and people would go see her.

When the gym wasn't so busy, she went inside with me, wandering around, hanging out with everybody. She was treated like a queen.

When I went mountain bike riding, I would set up all her stuff and chain her outside the van and she would just have her own little area at the trailhead in the parking lot. She had her own L.L. Bean memory-foam mattress and a rug for her water and toys.

When I found this sport, it wasn't as organized or professional. Everybody was just kind of winging it. You had a bunch of guys that liked to snowboard. They weren't going to these training facilities. They weren't going to these academies for snowboard cross. We were riding regular snowboards. I won my first World Cup on a K2 board that I got from John Schmoock, my local rep in the Midwest. Later in my career, we were all riding on custom-made boards from board makers, mostly in Switzerland. Suddenly we were on these rocket ships. The equipment changed; it became faster. These kids were training at such a young age, which lifted the talent level.

And I had to train even harder. Just to find an edge.

Every night in Marquette, after mountain biking and working out at the gym, I went to Lake Superior with Oakley to clean off and chill out. Literally. Lake Superior is known for staying cold all summer because it's so deep. We have amazing lakes in the Upper Peninsula, but nothing compares to Superior. Then, I relaxed by messing around on a Fliteboard, a battery-powered hydrofoil with a propeller. It looked like a surfboard that would rise out of the water. I would ride it out on the lakes and it just helped me to reset everything. It would make my mind relax and chill out.

But more than anything, it was just damn fun. I had a blast on it.

If you are gonna go on a crazy journey, you might as well have fun along the way.

All summer, I didn't do any construction. Didn't make any money. And spent days away from Landon. Calling it a sacrifice could never begin to explain it. But I was making a bet on myself. I was spending a lot of time in Marquette, but I didn't have enough money to stay in a hotel. So I decided to live out of my van.

I got teased: "You have turned that van into basically a one-bedroom house. It's kind of like RV life."

I was guilty as charged.

At first, I parked near the trailhead of the south trails in Marquette. But the cops woke me up and kicked me out of there at like 1:30 in the morning. I had to drive up to the grocery store parking lot and sleep there, which kind of sucked. Then I ended up finding a spot in Negaunee, at an old airport that was being developed. Nobody bothered me there. But I must have looked like some kind of crazy drifter, living in a 20-year-old van, a 2001 Ford Econoline.

I got the van from my brother, who had acquired it from our cousin—which was kind of a funny story. My brother got the van to pull his boat around. It was bright yellow. He put tape around it in stripes and then he hit it with black spray paint. So, when I got it, it looked like a bumblebee. But I got it for free, so I'm not complaining. The van was loaded with returnable cans, and Landon and I dug through it and found $500 of returnable beer cans.

Most of the time, I used it as my work van, stuffing all my concrete tools in it, driving from job to job. I kept pretty much everything right in the van. When Landon and I went camping, I would just back the van up to the garage, empty all the concrete tools out, throw a double mattress between the wheel wells and pull my queen-sized memory foam over the top of that. The van worked great, but it sounded kind of bad. It had a hole in the exhaust manifold and the passenger side was starting to rot off, so it didn't sound real nice.

But it still ran, and that was all that mattered.

It was a shitty van and sounded terrible, but it slept like it was first class, especially with Oakley right beside me.

———————

Over the years, people said I was making sacrifices to chase this Olympic dream. But I always thought of it the other way. My life was not on hold. My life revolved around a simple dream— winning an Olympic medal. So I lived out of a van and spent every waking hour training or recovering from training and I was pushing my body, trying to fight back Father Time.

Landon? Now that was the true story. He was the one truly making sacrifices. Because we didn't have much money. We had to live frugally, and I was away from him so much. That was the real sacrifice in my Olympic journey.

———————

As an older athlete, I had one mindset: it's easy to train on the days when you feel good and nothing hurts and you're healthy and everything is good. No problem. But it's not going to last forever. When you are getting older and you've had some injuries and your back is sore and your muscles are tight and your ankles hurt and your knees ache, it is so much harder to stay focused. To keep training. To stay motivated.

Of course, there were days when I got tired. When I was drained and sore and would get up and think, *I can't do this anymore.*

Absolutely.

If people say they don't have those days, they're lying. But when you feel like that, when you are faced with a decision—to train or not—that's when the great ones define themselves. There will be those days when you don't feel like it, when you're not feeling good, when you don't want to go to the gym, when you don't want to go out there and compete against yourself, but on those days, that's when you separate yourself from the others. Champions set themselves apart by doing it on the days they don't feel like doing it. So those are the days you have to push even harder, on those days when you don't want to put in the work, you've still got to put in the work. And if you can do it on those days, man, you got some good things coming your way.

———————

By fall, I was stronger, in great shape, but out of money and needed to go back out to Aspen to help my brother. We had my workout set up so that when I went to Aspen in the fall, I could continue to do my program. To keep grinding.

———————

Stressed about money and not sure how I was going to pay for everything, I started talking with KC Atanasoff, whose family owns Krist Oil Company, which was based in Iron River. Krist is a fourth-generation company that sells petroleum, propane, and convenience items at stores across Michigan, Wisconsin, and Minnesota.

"I have a lot going on in my personal life and I'm short on sponsorship," I told KC.

He was just 36 but seemed significantly older. We went to the same high school. He also played football, but a few years behind me. I had done some work for Krist when I was in high school. They had a big camp outside Iron River, and we'd go out there and get paid to clean up debris, cutting down trees that were dead or had become a hazard.

"Well, Nick, how can we help you?" KC said. "What do you need from me?"

He had an amazing idea.

"We're trying to get a loyalty-based program running within our company," he said. "It's an app that our customers sign up for and there's discounts associated. I can't think of a better person than you to help us promote loyalty."

I was all in.

"In exchange for, you know, our support, I would ask for a little bit of your time helping our marketing director," KC said.

Heck yeah. I loved the idea, and I loved the story behind the Krist Oil Company, because it was a pure Yooper story. It was about somebody chasing a crazy dream and taking chances. Basically, it was my story in the business world, from a different era. KC's great grandfather, Krist Atanasoff, came to the United States in 1909 from Southeastern Europe and purchased a candy store in the small town of Caspian in 1917. He operated the candy store for a few years, mostly serving miners. After prohibition ended in 1933, Krist bought a tavern across the street from the candy store. As automobiles became popular, he added gasoline pumps at the tavern, offering full-service fill-ups. Then, he started the Stambaugh Oil Company. But he died unexpectedly in 1956. His son Stanley purchased the remainder of the company from his family and changed the name from Stambaugh Oil Company to Krist Oil Company in remembrance of his father.

Nearly a half century later, Krist stores had spread all over the U.P.

KC was the fourth generation to work at the company.

"We can help you personally, but we also have a great vendor network," KC said. "We can reach out to these vendors, but I don't know how motivated they're going to be to jump on board. I don't know with COVID, and everything else that the world is enduring, how deep their marketing budgets are."

I loved the idea.

KC committed to helping me, but he also started contacting other companies to try to get me other sponsorships. And I don't think I could ever thank him enough. It was like getting a lifeline.

But KC helped me in so many other ways. It wasn't just money. It was countless little things.

One day, I sent him a text: "Do you guys make the firewood bundles? I ran out of sauna wood."

"How many you need?" he replied. "I'll get Dave Pellizzer to drop off tomorrow."

"I could come pick up so I can steam up tonight," I replied.

"Hold on a second," he replied. "I'll see if someone is there. I'm in Florida for flight training or I'd be there."

"Hell yeah," I wrote. "Where at?"

"I was in Texas last week, but now in Florida for additional event near Fort Myers," he responded.

"Dang," I wrote. "My buddy owns a bad ass race plane you should go for a ride in. That's in Orlando if you make it that way."

KC texted back: "Firewood: Kiel (my brother) is there now till around 8 PM. He'll get it loaded for you. He's there now. He knows you'll be calling."

Then, he added: "That would be cool in that plane…I'm down here each year for recurring training, so possibly next year. This year is hectic with garbled schedule from cancellations from COVID from the past two years. Please let me know that you've connected with Kiel."

"I'm calling now," I wrote.

Then, I texted again: "Gonna head down now."

He put in all that work for me. Just for a pallet of sauna wood. I could never thank him enough.

When I started snowboard cross, the sport was in a weird stage. I was the first jock snowboarder. The first traditional sports guy—a big football player and three-sport athlete. But most of the snowboarders were skinny little skateboarders. They had this attitude: *I'm here. I'm having fun. It's cool.*

I'm not knocking them. We were just different and we came from different places and had different mindsets. Back then, snowboarders were like, we don't need to train, we just do it. And that was the cool thing. To just show up and ride. That was how the coaches approached it, too. The coaches didn't act like high school football coaches, demanding excellence, holding you accountable. The coaches partied with us and made jokes at our expense. If you were on the team from the beginning and you were good, they let you get away with so much. Stuff that made the team culture hard to deal with. It wasn't ideal back in the early days but we were dominant, so things didn't change for a while. Everything was slow and easy and relaxed.

But that slowly started to change. I firmly believe the only way to get faster is to train to be fast. But I have to be honest; there was a time when I wasn't training as hard as I should have. I was doing the minimum. When you are young, you think you can get away with it. And when you do that, when you don't get the results you want, you start to learn that things are not gonna be very fun for you.

Every year, you find out you've got to do a little bit more and a little bit more, just to be able to do this. In order to be the best at something, you have to be borderline obsessed.

Not everybody believed in me.

When I told people I was training for the Olympics, I could see the doubt in their eyes.

Some said it to my face: "Do you really think you can make it?"

"At your age?"

I heard it in the tone of their voice.

"How old are you?"

"I'm 40."

"And you think you can make the Olympics?"

Few believed me. They thought I was crazy.

And I let that fuel me: *Don't believe in me? You are gonna see. Think I'm crazy? Well, yeah, I'm crazy.*

Because I had this amazing, massive dream, and I refused to give it up. I wasn't going to listen to the critics.

I was used to people doubting me.

So I refused to engage with them on social media, a lesson I wish everyone would learn.

If someone tells you you can't do this, let 'em think it. And prove 'em wrong with your action. Do not get into an argument with them on social media. Leave that negativity to them; let it ruin their life.

So I kept working, kept saving up money, kept making plans, and kept dreaming the most amazing dream.

On September 24, I got some great news.

KC sent me a text telling me the sponsorship was complete.

"Nick, confident that the check will be available Saturday. Please provide email address for me to communicate to our graphic design firm."

I responded: "Thank you so much for believing in and helping me finish this long career off with a bang. This will be just as tough as the last three Olympics, but because of this sponsorship, I can now focus 100% on preparation rather than stressing out about how I will cover my expenses. I look forward to sharing this story of support with all my following and just being a positive spokesperson for Krist Oil. It makes me very proud to partner with you guys and I will say again that this is because how hard you kids (we aren't that old brother) work for everything you have! Thanks for giving this blue-collar Olympian a more even playing field."

I typed out nine heart emojis.

———————

I was scheduled to go to Colorado in November for a snowboard camp when my brother Josh called, asking for some help.

"Could you come early and help us do some concrete work?" Josh asked. He was a general contractor in Colorado, building massive, expensive houses.

"Sure," I said.

We had to pour concrete in the snow, pushing to get a foundation in the ground so that we could be ready for the build in the spring. We ended up pouring till 10:30 at night with lights.

Josh said I was an animal with a shovel. We couldn't get the concrete pump truck close enough to reach the back of the foundation, so we had to add 60 feet of six-inch concrete hose and run that across the top of the forms. Josh and I were the ones who grabbed the end of the hose and dragged it around, late into the night.

The next day I was with the U.S. Snowboard Team training for the Olympics.

———————————

Maybe there is a giant universal lesson in that: sometimes you're gonna have to take a job in life that you don't like or that doesn't seem like it's lined up with your dream. Sometimes you've got to do whatever it takes. I always had to be a construction worker pouring concrete in the summer so that I could fund my dream in the winter. And again, it all started with being a Yooper. We were never going to accept the excuses. We were going to do whatever it took to get what we want.

People would always yell at me for wearing my Vancouver Olympics ring when I was pouring concrete. But I wore it on purpose. When I was pouring concrete, beat up and exhausted, I looked down and saw that thing staring back at me. Reminding me that my competitors didn't have to pour concrete—they were in the gym putting in the work. I figured they were working out when I was working a real job. So when I was done with a long day of concrete and wanted to relax and chill before bed, that ring reminded me that I didn't have that luxury. I needed to get my ass to the gym. And if I did that, and if I found success at the Olympics, maybe, just maybe, I wouldn't have to pour as much concrete in the future. Plus, if I took off my ring, I would have lost it.

———————————

Athletes find motivation in all kinds of places.

Six quarterbacks were drafted before the New England Patriots selected Tom Brady—a fact that always motivated him.

Michael Jordan got cut from his high school varsity team and was placed on junior varsity.

And I found motivation in that Olympic ring. Covered with concrete.

But there was something else—another slight.

Several months before the Winter Olympics, a large group of reporters and media members were invited to a summit to meet the top Olympic hopefuls. They would gather in one location for interviews and to take pictures to be used during the Olympic Games. It's where they got a lot of their preview material.

I was never invited to it. I was always overlooked. I was never one of the high-profile athletes, and I was always flying under the radar. It bummed me out a little, but it also always pushed me to show them to never forget about a Yooper.

Or you're going to get bit right in the ass.

I gave my body the best chance to win training in Marquette.

I filled my mind with confidence knowing I couldn't have trained harder.

So it was time to fix my eyes.

Leaving nothing to chance, I decided it was time to get my vision corrected. On October 21, I went to Salt Lake City for a couple days. I had PRK, a type of laser eye surgery similar to Lasik, done at the Moran Eye Institute. I wasn't sure how much of a difference it would make, but I knew it couldn't hurt. It helped that the U.S. Snowboard Team was willing to pay for it.

November 28, 2021
Zhangjiakou, China
World Cup

I shared some amazing news on Facebook.

"First race of the season and I'm so excited to land on the podium!" I wrote on Facebook, after taking third place in a snowboard cross competition held in China, on the same course where the 2022 Winter Olympics would be held in February. "The fact that it was on the Olympic course makes it that much sweeter. When you have days like today it makes all the sacrifices worth it! Thanks so much to everyone that believed in me and also thanks to everyone that didn't because you had a lot to do with it too."

A few days later, I sent a note to KC: "What a heck of a race Sunday. Big things happening brother. Thanks for believing in me."

I included the link to a story from Team USA. The headline read: "Nick Baumgartner Grabs Third Place at Snowboard Cross Olympic Venue."

The story was written by Bob Reinert, and it began, "It would seem that Nick Baumgartner has discovered something akin to the fountain of youth. Acting nothing like the 39-year-old he is, the three-time Olympian and member of the U.S. men's snowboardcross team rode to a third-place finish Sunday in the first Olympic test event at Secret Garden in Zhangjiakou, China."

I read the words and was getting pumped.

They had created a 4,110-foot-long course with 45 features—a slower course that suited an experienced rider like me. Best of all, organizers said it was nearly identical to the planned Olympic course.

KC wrote back: "Sounds good! We're all very proud of you! I want to find out how we can help you more and how to get another check to you. Your involvement with us has greatly helped us in our advertising initiative and we want to show that appreciation with additional support...Keep the drive up! You got this one!"

I was back on the podium.

KC was sending more sponsorship money.

And everything seemed to be aligned.

"Thanks so much KC," I responded. "Your support means the world to me and allows me to focus. Let's blow this crap out of the water. Night brother."

I returned to Iron River and kept trying to secure other sponsorships. An intriguing one was with Baja Vida, a company that made Baja Beef jerky. KC had the great idea to start selling the jerky in Krist Oil stores if they would sponsor me.

On December 7, I sent a text to KC: "Morning KC, I just got off the phone with Baja Beef jerky and want to do a text introduction for the two of you! I think he would be planning to call you at your earliest convenience, but I want to give you a heads up. I really appreciated your help with this and all your support. Obviously, you do what's best for you guys but to help me let him know that this is possible because of our relationship and who I am."

I included a winking emoji.

"You're the man. I can call if you have any questions or just let me know if the text introduction works for you."

COVID messed everything up.

When I went home for Christmas, I went into isolation because of COVID. I was afraid of being around everybody and picking up the virus and missing out on the Olympics. So even though it killed me, I had to stay away from my family during the holidays.

I spent 35 hours building a track around my house. My neighbors had to be looking at me and saying, "What is this guy doing? He's crazy."

I did that for multiple reasons. For one thing, it gave me a training track at my house. There was no way to get lazy and no excuses about not being able to train when you have a track right outside your front door. But I also did it for the mental side of things. When I was building that track, I was having fun, I was giggling. I was like a little kid again. That allowed me to keep my mind off the stress and the pressure and everything that could go through your head before a big event like the Olympics. When I was done, I had a great place to train. So it was a win-win. And I was just hoping to inspire somebody.

Also, it was just an insane workout, snowblowing and shoveling for that many hours. The sweat was a perfect addition to my daily workouts. I tried to explain it in an Instagram post: "I'm like a happy kid building a snow fort, plus I can't help but giggle when my neighbors drive by and look at me like I'm crazy," I wrote. "The question is…are you willing to do whatever it takes to achieve your dreams?"

My dreams were bigger than getting to the Olympics—I had already done that three times. The goal was to win a medal.

When I wasn't at my house, training on my own track, I went to Ski Brule and logged up to 50 runs a day—sometimes before noon, because Ski Brule was so small. I went up and down the run, up and down. Then, I got on the chairlift and people were like, "What is wrong with you, man? You're crazy. Like, just out here by yourself."

It was funny, riding the same short lift and taking the same run, over and over again. After every run I had 15-second conversations with the Lifties—the people running the chair lift. We would try to get a full conversation done in two sentences each.

These were just fun small-town things that I cherished. I mean, these people would work out in the cold all day, helping people onto the lift and making sure we could keep having fun. They played a big part in my journey and relationships. Smiles and awkward four-sentence conversations were funny and ridiculous but also something I really cherish looking back.

I was convinced that the Olympic course was going to be ideal for me. And when I was at Ski Brule, going up and down…up and down…I was imagining the Olympic course.

I felt so prepared. I was coming off two podiums, one on the Olympic course, feeling really good and ready to get there and make some noise.

In other years I went to the Olympics, I was always fighting for that last spot on the team. Even though I was in my prime, nothing was certain, and I had to keep fighting to make it.

But for the 2022 Olympics, I knew I was on the team because I was the top qualifier and had the most points. It felt way better. All the pressure melted away.

I had always struggled with nerves. But the only way to get rid of nerves is preparation. If you are prepared, and you've done everything in your power to be ready for what you're about to do, that is the only way to control those nerves.

And I felt so prepared for these Games.

So the nerves were gone.

On December 31, I wrote to KC, "Happy New Year KC. How's the holidays going? My coaches and I decided it was best if I skipped the next two races in Russia. The travel is a nightmare and with the COVID spike, we decided it was better for me to stay home and train here."

He responded less than two hours later: "Happy New Years, Buddy! Everything here is going great! We are anticipating that gold medal that you've worked your ass off for! Can't wait to see you wearing it! I can imagine that international travel is a horrid nightmare as of late, so I'm sure you're a bit relieved with the short time home! I hope you have a very nice New Year's holiday and I know that next year is going to be an awesome year for you. P.S.: We are still working with that Beef Jerky company on arranging it for our primary brand, so full steam ahead there! I hope they are showing you the respect for the lead in their sponsorship as I have dropped hints to it in our discussions with them."

I responded, "Much appreciated brother. Your support has been huge in helping me accomplish that goal. When do you guys start having it on the shelves and is it going in all the stores?"

"We need to figure a ton of stuff out yet with distribution so it will be a month or so, but it's coming, and it is going to be big for them. The holidays halted talks a bit, but they will resume shortly after the New Year. I will reinforce their mandatory sponsorship of you with their agreement to us as they are getting a ton of advertising with us and I told them we intend for you to be a part of that advertising initiative."

It was a crazy idea—get Baja Beef jerky into the Krist stores.

It helped Baja, it helped me, and it was a new product for Krist. Pure Yooper spirit, baby. Everybody helping everybody.

At the last minute, I had a few more sponsors jump on just before the Olympics to help support me. One of them was American Pavement Solutions out of Green Bay. It was crazy how that came together. I was flying from Chicago to Green Bay, and I happened to be on the same flight with the boss of one of my best friends from high school. Ten years earlier, we had tried to get them as a sponsor, but it didn't happen. But when we started talking again, they were like, alright, we need to revisit this. My friend hit him up and they said absolutely. And they helped out as well.

The more sponsors I had, the less pressure I felt about money and paying bills.

Man, everything was coming together.

CHAPTER 12

THE 2022 OLYMPICS

Packing for the 2022 Winter Olympics.

Passport. Computer. And the most important bag, filled with something I couldn't lose in transport—five handmade Oxess snowboards. Each one was 163 centimeters long with a black carbon fiber on the top sheet and a titanium layer to help with flex and stability in the corners. Shaped like an hourglass, with a skinnier waist than the top and bottom, it had a 10.7-meter side cut.

Pretty badass, high-tech, and fast—my own little rocket ships.

It's remarkable, really, when you consider where this sport began. Snowboarding actually started in Michigan with a troll—a guy named Sherman Poppen from below the Mackinac Bridge. In 1965, Poppen was living in Muskegon, a town in Western Michigan, and he needed to do something with his kids on a winter day. So, he bolted a pair of skis together and they rode it down the hill like a thin surfboard. He called it "snurfing."

Thankfully, the name didn't catch on. I can't imagine being called an Olympic Snurfboarder.

Sounds like I'd be blue or something, like one of the Smurfs.

They started holding snurfing competitions in Muskegon, Michigan, and one of the early snurfers was Jake Burton Carpenter.

He started making boards by hand in his garage, eventually starting the Burton Snowboards Company in 1977—four years before
I was even born. The first Burton snowboards had single-strap
bindings with a rope and handle attached to the nose.

After the rope and handle were long removed, I actually raced
Burton boards in 2009 and at the 2010 Olympics.

The next year, I switched to Oxess boards made by hand by
Marcel Brunner, a former cabinet maker from Switzerland who
founded the brand. Bruner put a lot of love, knowledge, and pre-
cision into making the fastest boards possible. I called him "The
Wizard" because he made boards that were special, specifically
made for snowboard cross. Specifically made for me. I was a little
bit heavier and bigger, so I needed a specific board built for me.

Essentially, I used the same Oxess model since 2011. But we
still tweaked it to make it better and better.

Even though I packed five Oxess boards for the Games, they
were prepared differently. I had a board just for training—just an
old, retired board from a couple of years prior. The other boards
had different grinds—the structure on the bottom that helps break
the suction, allowing water and snow to escape, preventing the
board from forming a suction cup to the snow. If I had to guess,
I had probably 25 to 30 snowboards in my basement. I could sell
them, but I would rather let people borrow them and then tell
them how to get them from The Wizard, to try to help his business. Besides, those boards still held a strong sentimental value
to me because I had so much success on them, helping me win
a race or qualify for an Olympics.

Truly, I believed they were the best boards in the world—and
one of the secrets to my success over the years.

For the Olympics, I planned to use a board with a cold base
on it, and it was ground by my old wax tech, Andy Buckley, who

had waxed my boards forever. Buckley played such an important role behind the scenes. He was my wax tech from late 2007 until he retired in 2018 to work back home so he could spend more time with his family. He had earned it.

But he still ground my boards.

Next stop?

Basically, it was like Christmas morning for Olympians—time to open all kinds of presents.

As Olympians, we were given thousands of dollars' worth of swag from Nike, Ralph Lauren, and Skims, and we picked it up before flying to Beijing. It was like a wild shopping spree, although everything was free. We had our choice of winter jackets, gloves, boots, winter pants, sweatpants, hats, and shoes. Almost everything was red, white, and blue.

We got a Ralph Lauren Opening Ceremony outfit: pants, jacket, and cool white boots.

There was a Closing Ceremony outfit: sweater, pants, and a thick, comfy jacket. An outfit to wear during media appearances, like press conferences: jacket, pants, and shoes. Stuff to just wear around the Olympic Village: T-shirts, hats, custom sweaters. When you unpacked it all and spread it across a room, the amount of swag was mind-blowing. But I was used to it. We got the same kind of swag at every Olympics. In other years, I ended up giving away some of it to family and friends. But most went to people for cancer benefits or to help raise money for a fellow Yooper when life was beating them up and they needed help paying for hospital bills or maybe a house fire.

But there was one other outfit. A special one. The only one I cared about. The only one I truly dreamed of wearing: a specific outfit to wear at the medal ceremony.

Preferably, while getting a gold.

February 5, 2022
Beijing, China
2022 Winter Olympics

The media was always grabbing a storyline and running with it or pumping up the same high-profile athletes.

Before the Beijing 2022 Olympics, there were a couple of big-name stories: Shaun White was shooting for his fourth gold medal in halfpipe snowboarding, and Mikaela Shiffrin went to Beijing trying to win her third gold medal in alpine skiing.

I was mentioned in some preview stories, mainly because the writers were having fun with my age, pointing out the extremes on the team. The youngest member of Team USA was Alysa Liu, who was born on August 8, 2005. She would be 16 years, 6 months old when she competed in figure skating, which was just stunning to me. I mean, my son was just two years older than her. At the other end of the spectrum, I stood alone, the oldest member of Team USA. I had turned 40 on December 17, 2021. Hard to believe; I had always assumed a curler would always grab the graybeard title.

Gotta love outlasting the curlers.

The media pointed out several recent examples of older athletes winning at the highest level: Tom Brady had won his most recent Super Bowl at 43, Phil Mickelson won the PGA Championship at 50, and just a week earlier, surfing legend Kelly Slater had won a major contest only days before his 50th birthday.

So, you're telling me there's a chance? Ha. Of course; there is always hope!

I loved it. Loved the idea of being called the old guy. Because there was one thing I relished more than anything: beating the crap out of the youngsters half my age.

During interviews or even in casual conversations, some people were always dancing around the age issue, almost as if they were saying, "We don't want to call you old. We don't want to offend you by pointing out your age."

But I didn't care. It was part of my story, and I embraced it. At some point, everybody is going to deal with aging. We can't run from it. Or even limp away from it with a cane. We just do our best to delay it as long as we can.

Another predictable, every-four-years storyline—at least in the general media—focused on athletes who didn't make it to the Games. At the 2022 Games, the poster child for his surprising absence was my friend Alex Deibold.

Alex had won bronze at the 2014 Sochi Games and would have had a chance to medal in China. But days before Beijing, he crashed during qualifying at a World Cup event and was replaced by Jake Vedder, a 23-year-old, also from Michigan.

So, at a press conference previewing the snowboarding action, I wasn't surprised to be asked about Alex.

As I started to answer the question, the emotion bubbled to the surface, and I stopped midsentence. "Sorry, I'm kind of a crybaby all the time," I told reporters. "But it's tough. Tough not seeing him."

I was supposed to room with Alex in Beijing, and I was seriously bummed for him.

Actually, I was in Italy, too, at that same competition as Alex, the one where he got hurt. But I got through it and stayed healthy. Knock on wood. I felt bad for Alex, happy for Vedder. This was

Vedder's first Olympics, my fourth, and I was old enough to be his father.

Snowboarding could be so cruel. You had to put yourself in dangerous situations to be prepared, living on the edge, pushing the limits, even during an Olympic year, while trying to stay safe and healthy.

Tricky, to say the least.

"If you play it safe and you take it easy, you're not going to be ready for the Games," I told reporters. "He was just out there preparing, getting ready to come here and do the best he could. He had a crash that scared us big time. We're just thankful that he's OK."

The more I talked, the more emotional I got, and the water-works hit again. I began to tear up. "Bummed enough to see him not be able to give it one more shot," I said, choking up. "We're going to do it for ourselves and our families, but absolutely, we're going to do this for Alex Deibold as well."

At every Olympics, reporters seemed to cling to one big focus or overarching storyline. Before this one, the big question revolved around the tricky, unpredictable conditions. Reporters kept asking questions about the weather, wondering if we trained differently to prepare for it. But I thought that was funny, and I was thinking, *I grew up riding in tricky, nasty conditions. In the Midwest, when it gets cold out, we ride on man-made snow, and it gets icy.*

If you can ride in those conditions, at Ski Brule or even on the track around my house, you can ride anywhere. When you go somewhere like Colorado or Utah, and the snow is perfect, it's easy. All these youngsters, who have never faced anything less than ideal conditions? Sure. It might be hard for them. But I'm a Yooper. That was one of the huge advantages that came from training at Ski Brule. I've been preparing for these conditions my whole life. The snowboard conditions in Michigan can be brutal. It can be bitterly cold in the Upper Peninsula, and the snow can be awful. Or the conditions can change suddenly because of sudden snowfall. I'm not saying that to complain. Actually, it turned into one of my strengths, having the ability to handle any conditions.

So, heck yes, I feel prepared. This is my race to win. I go into everything thinking I'm going to win.

This Olympics was, by far, the strangest for me for several reasons.

First, I had a new roommate. For 15 years, I roomed on the road with Jonathan Cheever—a snowboarder who worked as a plumber to support his career and pay his bills. So, we came from similar situations. We joined the team at the same time. We had come out of the same training camp. We got along the best, and the coaches put us together. A match made in Union Heaven. The concrete guy and the plumber—what a pair.

He was a four-time national champion who had appeared in 10 Winter X Games and earned five World Cup podiums. But Cheever retired. So, I was supposed to room with Alex Deibold. But when he got hurt, they put me with Vedder—a 23-year-old rookie who came from a different generation and was young enough to be my son.

Some people might think that it was weird to stay in a room with one of your competitors. It might be hard to imagine the starting quarterback from one NFL team sharing a room with the starting quarterback from another team, especially the night before a big game. But it was never like that in snowboarding. There was never much drama or hard feelings, staying with guys we competed against. We all got along, for the most part, and we were used to it. We were still part of a team at the end of the day, even though we competed against each other.

To us, it just seemed normal.

But there were several other things that made this Olympics seem so strange. My family wasn't allowed to attend because of tight COVID-19 restrictions. Foreign spectators were prohibited from attending because of the worldwide pandemic, and only specially invited and screened Chinese visitors could even go to events. Athletes were basically locked in our rooms. Hotels and venues seemed like islands, separated from ordinary Chinese by temporary fences and checkpoints.

And everyone in the Olympic bubble received a daily test for Covid.

At my first three Olympics, I was able to experience the full circus. I went wherever I wanted and did whatever I wanted, and I loved it. Like hanging out with NHL superstars and partying until 5 AM—it was amazing to meet elite athletes from around the world, getting to know them, while trying to get to as many events as possible. But 2022 was strange and different. The Olympics brought together 2,897 athletes in seven sports and 15 disciplines, but the whole event felt so much smaller because we weren't allowed to go around or hang out with anybody.

Maybe that wasn't all bad. Maybe that was a blessing for me, because it eliminated distractions. We weren't allowed to do crazy things or go to big events. As an aging athlete, I needed to be laser-focused, and the restrictions forced me to focus on what I could do, which was pretty much nothing. I competed, returned to my apartment, and ate at the cafeteria, separated from other athletes by Plexiglass dividers.

I used the extra time to recover. Get massages. Go to physical therapy sessions. And get my mind right. I did everything possible to make sure that when it was my time to compete, I was going to be ready. But I have to admit that I felt bad for the younger athletes who were at their first Olympics. For some, it could be their only Olympics, and they missed so much of the experience. They didn't get to see the craziness.

Still, as members of Team USA, we found ways to be cooler than everybody else. We got out of the apartments and rode around in the freezing cold on these sick little bikes with baskets on them. All the other countries were trying to steal our bikes.

Just cracked me up.

I was joking with people, "Listen, if you guys keep making these courses slower and not as crazy, I'm going to be able to do this until I'm 50."

There was a part of me that didn't like that I was still able to compete as a 40-year-old. At some point, I should show up, look at the course, and say, "Nah. That's it. No more. There's too much risk. I'm too old. I can't be doing this. I'm tapping out."

That was where we wanted to see this sport go. I wanted this sport to be badass. I wanted all this cool stuff—huge jumps and high speeds. But that wasn't happening.

So, um, "Here I am! Going for another Olympics!"

But there is a big difference between a badass course…and a dangerous one.

In 2018, at the PyeongChang Games, the course was dangerous. If you compared the 2018 course to the one they set up in 2022, it was a night and day. The size of the jumps and the air time was completely different.

In 2018, it was a gnarly course, and we were jumping 80 feet. People started wiping out and ending up on crutches.

But the pendulum had swung the opposite direction for 2022.

They started making these tracks smaller and safer—not exactly where we envisioned this sport going. We wanted to see big gnarly shit that only a handful of people would even attempt to race. We don't want just *anyone* to be able to come in and race in this sport. We wanted to make it so that they had to work up to that position.

But the organizers thought they knew better than us. So, the courses got easier.

At X Games, back in the day, we were jumping 130 feet at 60 miles an hour. But at these 2022 Olympics, there weren't really any big jumps that were comparable. The course was set up for slower speeds with no real big jumps. It was made to create tighter racing, crazier racing. Not gnarly.

I was the first to admit that I benefitted from that huge change. Because it played into my strength. For my whole career, I've always been very good at gliding, leaving my board flat and not edging at all, which allows you to go faster.

———————

Over the years, so many other things had changed, too.

Early in my career, we raced four snowboarders at a time in FIS (International Ski and Snowboard Federation) competitions. Then, we always raced six at a time at X Games. So, FIS went to six people at a time for the 2014 and 2018 games. And yes, it did make things more exciting, which was what they wanted. But that changed how many advanced. When you went from 32 to 48 in the field, you were getting all those people that couldn't qualify for the 32. Maybe they shouldn't be out there racing. Maybe they needed to put in some more time.

Suddenly, there was a bigger chance that some of these kids were a liability out there. Some of them didn't know what they were doing and could take you out, or crash into you, or just do something stupid. I didn't like that. When you limit the finals to 32, you're getting only the best guys. You respect each other. Because the people who make it have experience. They know the risk involved. But when you start letting in people that take crazy risks, that's how people end up getting hurt.

February 10, 2022

I felt like an idiot.

"Look how stupid we look," I said to one of the administrators, a former Italian racer and FIS employee. Before racing in the snowboard cross men's individual race, I was wearing my official Team USA racing suit, and I felt like a silly weirdo. Instead of wearing a cool baggy snowboard outfit, they forced us to wear skintight racing suits that made us look like somebody dressed up like a superhero on Halloween—or, even worse, a downhill skier.

Nothing against skiers, but we are snowboarders. The cool guys on the mountain. We wanted to have our own sport, do it our own way, and not follow in their footsteps. That is exactly why snowboarding started. There will always be this ongoing joke about who is cooler. Snowboarders say, "If it were easy, they would call it skiing," or, "Twice the edges, half the fun." We were the rebels. The cool kids in the back of the room. The outcasts who blazed a new way to look at the mountain.

"Look what you did to us," I continued, giving him some crap.

Snowboarders have always had a gentleman's agreement that your pants should be baggy enough to, pulling from the side of your leg, stretch out as far as the width of a credit card.

Don't break the freakin' credit card rule!

We always had the ability to police this rule, holding people to a certain standard, because two of our teammates, Seth Wescott and Nate Holland, were given the power to invite athletes to the X Games. They earned that from their success and dominance in snowboard cross. Nate was very outspoken and loved to ruffle feathers. It sucked when he pointed his attack at you, which he often did with me because we butted heads. But it was hilarious when it was directed at other teams. He made sure that everybody knew that if you wore skinny pants at any race during the year that you would be ineligible to compete at X Games.

That allowed the U.S. riders to dictate what people wore.

"Well, there's no rule for it," the organizer said.

"Don't tell me there's not a rule," I shot back. "There's a clear rule, you just don't want to police it."

I've been competing for 17 years. Don't tell me about the rules.

I burst out laughing and walked away smirking. I was just messing with him, giving him some crap—serious about wanting to send a message about these ridiculous suits but not really ticked off. Times change. I wasn't going to let it ruin my day.

I always messed with people before I raced. It was how I stayed loose.

On one of the biggest days of my life, before competing in the individual men's race, I was feeling great, having a good time, keeping it lighthearted, and joking around with people. If there is one thing I've learned, I was far more successful when having fun.

———————

We went through our inspection and did our warm-up laps. Those went well—I was flying. I felt fast. The speed was there, and I felt good. I figured that I had a great chance to get to the final round, a great chance to medal. I just needed to stay alive.

The first round went well. I advanced. That's the secret to any race. Just keep advancing. I went out and showed my speed.

The next round? Ugh. It couldn't have gone any worse. In my quarterfinal, I went up against Austria's Julian Lüftner, Japan's Yoshiki Takahara, and Vedder—my roommate. But I made a small mistake, and that was it.

I was knocked out and broke down in an emotional interview with NBC after my quarterfinal run.

And the video started bouncing around the world on the internet.

CHAPTER 13

A NEW BEGINNING

February 10, 2022
Zhangjiakou, China
2022 Winter Olympics

Sad. Upset. Frustrated. Unbelievably disappointed.

While dealing with the disappointment of the individual race, and hearing rumblings that I might have a shot at being in the mixed team relay—*you can't believe it, not until it happens*—one of the things that helped me get my head screwed on straight was getting messages from friends and family in the U.P.

On February 10, at 11:50 PM, KC wrote me a note that I will always cherish:

"Nick, I know you're consumed with the Games, so I don't want a reply," he wrote.

"In the wake of yesterday's event, I felt it was important to write, letting you know how extremely proud we are of YOU here back home. I know that you're experiencing the feelings of the understandable disappointment, but know that to us, your community, and your fans, it is more than an event that makes Nick Baumgartner. You have brought great honor to our small northern town. You have achieved something impossible for most. You have positively impacted many lives throughout the area and instilled inspiration that has transpired into a sense of community, united, all surrounding your accomplishments. Your merits will likely never be forgotten. We know how dedicated you are. We can only begin to imagine the amount of work you have invested. Especially to this year's events in particular. I am so very honored to be a small part of this great venture of yours."

I read the note, and it lifted me up.

And I got several just like it.

Everyone said: "Keep your head up. What you've done is amazing. You didn't let anyone down. You crushed it."

———————

The whole experience was a huge lesson to me.

And I started realizing something: *You can't let one failure sabotage the next opportunity. So, learn what you can from it, leave the negative behind and take the positive.*

As the messages kept coming, and I realized the amazing people in my life, I found another lesson: *Surround yourself with good people. No one finds success alone, ever. You have to surround yourself with people who lift you up and build you up and make you a better person. Because sometimes you're not able to pick yourself up on your own. There will be times where you feel like you're broken, and you can't get it done, you can't move forward, and you will need your friends to encourage you.... Don't ever give up. Never. If you're going to dream big, you're not going to do it alone. You're gonna need to have a support system, people that push you to want to do better, and to help pick you up when things don't go your way.*

All these people kept encouraging me, kept pumping me up, and the voice in me grew stronger: *You can't quit. You can't sell yourself short. You can't give up on your dreams; you got to keep fighting for what you want. And when something bad happens, and you're devastated, and you take a second and take it all in, let those emotions come through. Learn from that failure and leave all the negative behind because it's in the past, there's nothing you can do about it. My whole life, I've been preaching that you can learn from your failures. So this is the moment. Learn from it. Focus on what's ahead of you.*

I was so focused on my individual race that I wasn't even thinking about the mixed-team relay. Never crossed my mind. Before the Olympics, we had a meeting to discuss how the team would be picked, but I didn't pay attention to it.

Because I wasn't focused on it.

Vedder, my roommate, did a great job in his first Olympics. I figured he would get one of the spots. But everybody started telling me that the United States would get two teams in the relay.

"Do we?" I asked. "OK, well, all right, we better double check and make sure. What's going on?"

One of my coaches confirmed it for me: "We get four people, but we don't know who we're gonna team together."

I was devastated after my individual race. The whole world saw it. I was crying, and all of my emotions came pouring out on national TV.

But my emotions were bouncing all over the map. I was actually happy for Austria's Alessandro Haemmerle, who won the men's race. I was so proud of him. I had raced against this kid for years and I've watched him grow up. For several years, he never won, never even advanced through the first round of one of our races for an entire season. But I saw him battle through it, even when he wasn't having success. I respected him so much for how he handled those struggles and I tried to mentor him. I wasn't even sure if he was going to quit before his success started. His brother decided to hang it up and go to school to become a doctor.

But Haemmerle decided to keep fighting for it, and the next season he started winning everything.

I had total respect for him. Was so happy that he was finding success. When I meet someone who has fought to get what they want, I am so honored. It takes a lot of guts and a lot of bravery to keep fighting when things don't go your way.

———————

Before officially naming the relay teams, the coaches were worried about my state of mind. "We have to make sure that you're over that," they said. "That devastation."

"I'm good," I said.

I was dealing with it. It was a heck of a lot easier to handle, knowing I had a chance to keep racing. We tried to get a relay into the Olympics in 2010. My coach for most of my career, Peter Foley, was the one who helped put it in motion and presented it to the International Olympic Committee (IOC). But we could never get traction with it. Nothing happened until somebody came up with a slightly different idea.

What if we put together a relay team with a man and a woman?

They were like, *Oh, hell yeah, we want that.*

Mixed-team snowboard cross is a relay-style event with the winner determined by total time. Four teams race at once. The guys go first, busting ass down the course, and the results determine when the starting gates open for their female teammates. If you build a one-second lead in the men's race, the first woman would be given a one-second lead in her race.

So I tried to convince the coaches: *I'm good. Seriously. I'm over it.*

———————

Finally, the coaches let me know they picked me to be in the mixed-relay race and were pairing me with Lindsey Jacobellis. I was relieved, but it really wasn't a surprise to me. Because it made so much sense.

This snowboard cross course at Genting Snow Park was built for us. It was a slower course, almost 1,400 meters long. It started at an altitude of 2,046 meters and gradually dropped 167 meters through the rollers and it reached 1,879 meters at the finish. The slower the course, the more it rewarded experienced riders. And I felt really comfortable on it after placing third in the men's big final at the World Cup in 2021.

When you race at a slower speed, everything gets compacted and it becomes tight racing. That forces you to make a series of split-second decisions that I've made a million times. My sport was so unpredictable. But I've been doing it for 17 years, and I could kind of predict what was going to happen. That gave me a tremendous advantage, especially on courses with tight racing.

This course had a little of everything. It required a technical start—and Lindsey and I both had strong technique.

It offered some passing opportunities—and I felt my passing had improved dramatically over the years.

It offered drafting opportunities—and the more experience you have, the better you get at drafting. The more courage you have.

It had some jumps, but nothing huge—and I was comfortable on jumps going all the way back to Iron River when my brother showed me how to use that football power.

More than anything, it required finesse and technical ability—and that's where we had the best advantage. I was paired up with the GOAT. I was thrilled and relieved.

Suddenly, I had a chance at redemption.

———————

This was Lindsey's fifth Olympics, and she was the best racer of her generation. Her list of accomplishments was amazing: five individual world titles, 10 individual X Games, and she killed it on the World Cup scene, climbing onto 52 podiums and winning a staggering 30 times.

I had traveled with her for 17 years, and we were pretty tight. Throughout our career, we had been through highs and lows together. She was like family to me. Like another younger sister.

Like me, she had struggled at the Olympics. In 2010, she swerved off course in a semifinal heat and missed the final. In 2014, she stumbled and missed the final again. And in 2018, she finished fourth.

It had been 16 years since she had climbed on an Olympic podium after earning a silver in 2006. Few had let her forget that 2006 race. She was in first place, cruising to a gold medal, and she did a famous snowboard trick called a method, just to put an exclamation point on it. It was sick. It looked awesome. But she tweaked it a little too hard, and she ended up falling down. She scrambled to her feet as quickly as possible but had to settle for second. Then, after falling at X Games, the media tore her apart for years, saying mean things about her.

On ESPN, Michael Wilbon and Tony Kornheiser spent a segment having a debate about Lindsey. I saw a video clip and it couldn't have been more wrong.

"Is Lindsey Jacobellis the least clutch athlete in the history of sports or just the most unlucky?" Kornheiser asked.

It irked me watching it. What a horrible lie and a ridiculous statement.

"No, I'm not going to call her that," Wilbon said. "The speeds in which these skiers are traveling, and she had this wipe out. I mean, her head winds up bouncing off the ice and allowing her to finish in second place. I'm not gonna call her some choke artist. I don't know skiing enough to be out here, taking tough stands."

"It's a made-up sport," Kornheiser said. "She gaffed in the Olympics when she tried to be a hot dog. She didn't try to be a hot dog here in this X Games nonsense, whatever it is, but I think that this makes her even more famous because she's the anti–Mariano Rivera. She cannot close."

"Oh, stop it," Wilbon said.

Clearly, they didn't know her, and I was so frustrated for her.

To me, it boggled my mind that they would say mean things about her. To call our sport "made up." Like every other sport wasn't made up—hey, I know, take a ball and a hoop. Let's call it basketball!

They were just ripping X Game athletes. Showing us no respect. Just crazy. But to see her keep fighting through that? I mean, what an inspiration. She was a bulldog on the racecourse. To be teamed up with her—and have a chance to come up clutch and stick it to the media—was amazing.

Early in my career, I used to be amped up all the time. I'd approach each race with a frenetic desire: *I got to win, I got to win, I got to win.*

But I approached the team race differently than an individual race. I always did better in team races, because I didn't feel any pressure in them. Besides, I was paired with the greatest female snowboard cross racer of all time.

Now if I made a little mistake, I had a little cushion. Somebody who could help me make up for it. Lindsey was so talented. But she also had a tremendous amount of experience to handle any situation.

The other reason the coaches put us together? Because we could handle any weather conditions, and weather reports suggested that new snow was coming.

If it snowed, or if the weather changed suddenly, we knew that it was going to take some smart racing to win that race.

———————

The Olympic Games are so many things to different people. To some, it is a TV event—almost like a nightly soap opera. To others, it is a battle between countries for the medal count. To others, it's like a reality TV show that plays out every day for a few weeks.

And this Olympics started off with some surprising twists.

Mikaela Shiffrin crashed 10 seconds into the giant slalom, an event she had won at the 2018 Olympics in Pyeongchang. Russian star figure skater Kamila Valieva, the gold-medal favorite in the women's figure skating, had tested positive for a banned substance. And Shiffrin did not finish in the slalom—probably her best event—another stunner. Shaun White, a three-time gold medalist, was competing in his fifth Olympics. But he took fourth in the halfpipe.

Basically, the U.S. was floundering.

Nothing was going right.

Not until Lindsey won the women's snowboard cross—the first American gold of the Games.

So, Mr. Kornheiser, I guess she *can* close!

February 11, 2022
Zhangjiakou, China

Then, everything seemed to turn upside down, and the Olympics took on a completely different tone.

Callan Chythlook-Sifsof, a member of the 2010 Olympic team, made a series of Instagram posts that accused snowboarding coach Peter Foley of sexual harassment and said that he had "taken naked photos of female athletes for over a decade."

The fallout was immediate and intense.

First, Foley denied the allegations, and U.S. Ski & Snowboard opened an investigation. The allegations were serious, and it was right to investigate them.

But it left us in a strange situation, to be on a team whose coach was accused of something so serious, while the competitions continued.

Personally, I had a complicated relationship with Foley, which changed over time. When I first joined the team, I was like the outsider coming in. And I remember an X Games—I think it was 2009—when he wouldn't really give me much time or advice and wouldn't bother to coach me even though I was on the team. He wasn't giving me any help to get better on the course. For me, it was frustrating. So I gave a pass to my brother and I made him go down and stand near Foley and listen to what he was telling Nate Holland and Seth Wescott.

My brother would call me on my cell phone and relay that information to me.

I get it. I was an outsider. Sometimes I rubbed people the wrong way with my loud personality. You had to prove yourself or earn it. But it was still weird.

When I first met Foley, I thought he was a terrible coach. He was so different than the coaches I had worked with in the Upper Peninsula, like Coach Kralovec, Coach Greenlund, or Coach Berutti, or my coaches at Northern.

But over time, I thought Foley had turned into an awesome coach. And it was so hard to explain why that changed. When I started, it was a completely different culture on the team—it was

filled with "snowboarder cool guys." We would show up at a race—
Here we are, we're having fun. And we're doing good. Everyone
would party, and then we would just go out and win.

We were on the podium every race—at least one, if not two, of
us. And that was just on the men's side. Lindsey was always on the
podium on the women's side, so we always had that side covered.

We were dominant. And it was an incredible experience.

There seemed to be a prevailing attitude: if it's not broken,
don't fix it.

But the rest of the world started to catch up, and Foley changed,
too. I don't know if it was the pressure, or what, but obviously
there was definitely some personal growth there. From the time
he started coaching me to the time he stopped during the 2022
Olympics, he became a completely different coach. He became
very good at learning how to make the team better, working on
his issues and improving the team culture to help us. His growth
as a coach was phenomenal.

After the news broke, Foley definitely separated himself from
us because he didn't want to be a distraction for us. He knew
enough not to bring that into our world right before a race and
make it a big fiasco. He was not allowed into the athletes' village
for a film review before the mixed team finals.

That was actually a big deal.

Because Foley had created an incredible video system to prepare us for racing, using technology to give us the best chance to
win. He was the best coach we had at breaking down video and
helping us learn from the training runs.

Before every race, Foley would set up two cameras on a course,
one filming the start and the other filming as much of the course
as possible, usually from a long distance away. Sometimes he'd go
across the valley to get to a point where he could zoom in and get
as much of the course as possible. He also went through countless

hours of training to operate a drone so he could get a better angle to film. That gave us a cool side benefit, amazing film to share on social media to help us get sponsorships.

It was funny; for all these years, when we would show up at an event, Foley would set up this thing that looked like a weather station. But it was a portable Wi-Fi system that he set up on the mountain. Whenever he filmed something, it went off that Wi-Fi system and immediately went to our iPads at the top of the course.

I would go down the course, go back to the top, and watch my run instantly. We were the only team to have this technology for many years. Eventually, I think a few other teams got it. But it was such a huge advantage for most of my career.

Other teams tried using an iPad to film their runs. Then their athlete would get to the top and watch the run on the iPad, but that meant they weren't filming the next race on that same iPad. It made it very inefficient.

Because we always filmed the other top riders as well, I could either watch myself or study another racer who was doing it better. Whoever was racing fast, Foley was filming them. And I could watch it, figure out what I was going to do differently, and jump right in the gate and do it.

Then, Foley took it to another level.

Everybody in the whole field was wearing transponders, so we knew everybody's time and we knew who was going fast on different sections of the course. Maybe the fastest start was by someone from Austria or France. Foley would take video of the fastest person at the start and overlay video from my start over the top of the fastest start. So it looked like you could see two people on the course, but it's two different videos. You could see how much that person beat me in this section, and how much I made up in the next section.

We could get really nerdy about it. That was the one thing about Peter Foley that was just above and beyond anyone else. He was so nerdy about these kinds of things, and he would give us a technical advantage over everyone else because of our video system. He had put in so much time and effort, building these overlays for every rider. Just so we could see how we compared against the fastest riders.

Sometimes riders from other teams would come up to us and say, "What in the hell? What is that weather station Foley keeps putting up?"

And we said, "It's so we can watch video immediately. And we're loving it."

The technology allowed us to find the fastest lines to take down the course, especially during time trials. Obviously that line was different when you added three or five people to the mix. If I tried to take the fastest line, which was higher in turn one, now they were all going to go to the inside and pass me and bully me out of the way.

So, we went through video sessions, trying to come up with different plans. We'd talk about what could happen on course. We'd watch everybody's training and debate the best strategies. It gave us a huge advantage over the rest of the world. It was quite impressive. No one else had that as long as we did.

Rob Fagen, who became our interim coach, had a different skill. He could look at a course and know the fastest lines without actually watching anybody ride. He could just see the line. He raced boarder cross for many years, and he was actually in my first Olympic heat of my life. He beat me.

I had been a snowboarder for just as long as him, but I didn't have his skill to look at a course and see the fastest line. What he did was quite impressive. I had so much confidence in him. When he told you something, all right, that was it.

So, when we did our video review, it was with Rob instead of Peter.

When we showed up to the venue to get our boards ready to go up and train, Foley was already up there. He had already set up the Wi-Fi system. He was already in position to get us all the video we needed. He had his radio and still was able to relay everything like normal.

––––––––––––

Thinking back, I will always be impressed and amazed by how Foley made sure his situation didn't affect our performances. To me, that shows how much he had grown as a person and as a coach. He went from a coach who I didn't fully respect, much less like, to one of the best coaches I have ever had in any sport. But there was another lesson that could be taken from this.

In my view, he made mistakes in how he coached me early in my career. But we all make mistakes in life. And I have always preached that as long as you learn from a mistake, you will never make it again. Use it to help you grow and become a better person. That is called being human. We all make mistakes and that is usually how we learn the most.

By the 2022 Olympics, I respected Foley so much because of the growth he made and the person he became. That is not meant as a statement about the accusations.

I'm just making it clear how I saw so much change in him with how he coached me and how much I respected him by the time this all went down.

––––––––––––

A thick, wet snow had fallen throughout the morning. It covered the course and slowed everything down. Lindsey and I worked with Rob and our teammates, Faye Gulini and Jake Vedder, to determine the best lines. Then, we went through a training run together. At the third feature, I flew up and landed on my ass, and I had to get up laughing.

Lindsey also made a huge mistake, and we were way behind Jake and Faye by the end.

We got to the bottom and we were like, "Well, we're glad we got that out of the way."

"Nick, we don't want aggressive Nick," one of my coaches said. "We want the guy up here smiling, having fun, cracking jokes. That's the guy we need."

"OK, that's the guy you are gonna get," I said.

When I was smiling and having a good time, not worried about anything, I always had a better chance of winning.

So I was at the top before the team race. I was having fun. All the pressure was off me.

The conditions were tricky because it started snowing. Everything got more complicated, more dangerous when the snow was falling.

In the quarterfinals, I was stuck behind Adam Lambert in the beginning before Australia's Cameron Bolton passed both of us. But I was able to pass Lambert and secure second. That forced Lindsey to start in second for her portion of the race, and she avoided two crashes from Australians Josie Baff and Belle Brockhoff to win the race. Brockhoff was taken off the course by stretcher and rushed to the hospital for precautionary neck scans.

That delayed the semifinals for 15 minutes.

In the semifinals, I got off to a great start with Omar Visintin, and we finished in a virtual tie. That just meant Jacobellis didn't have an advantage in the women's race. She sat comfortably behind Michela Moioli and they both progressed to the big final.

Before the final round, NBC was taking video of me at the top.

"The team race is a completely different atmosphere," I said, looking at the camera. "You can see all the athletes are just having fun."

I spread my arms out and smiled.

"You see better riding when that happens."

I bent down, zipped my bag, and screamed, "Yahoo!"

Another huge smile. Being loud and obnoxious. As always.

I was so excited, so happy.

Lindsey and I walked toward the top, our boots crunching on the snow.

"Let's go, stallion," I said and patted her on the back.

I zipped my coat. She leaned into a blue fence, her foot tapping up and down, rocking with the music, and she started bopping back and forth. I did the same. She turned and looked at me, raising both hands above my head, pumping her arms back and forth like we were on a dance floor.

I started fist pumping the wax techs—we have the best in the world. "Give me some of that lovin'!" I said.

I gave Lindsey a hug.

"Redemption!" I screamed and pumped both fists.

I was full of confidence. I had prepared for this moment for my entire lifetime.

For the entire year.

From Marquette to Ski Brule.

I grabbed my board. "Let's go!"

Linds followed me to the start area, and I got into position. I took a couple of deep breaths. Looked back and pointed at her.

"Let's go, baby!"

"Yeah!"

In the starting gate, I stood next to Eliot Grondin from Canada, the guy who had taken second place in the individual race. Next to him was Omar Visintin, from Italy, the guy who had won the bronze medal in the individual race.

And I thought, *This is my chance to prove the doubters wrong. To prove to everybody that all the training was worth it. To prove that I am racing fast. To prove that if I would have made it to the finals of the individual race, I could have won a medal. Could have won it all. I've lost repeatedly for 17 years. I've lost over and over and over and over again. But each time, I didn't quit; I kept going. I took that loss and learned from my mistakes.*

I just wanna beat these kids. I want to prove all my sacrifices have been worth it.

I knew all of my competitors. I had been studying them for years. I had raced against them and watched them on Foley's video system, studying their techniques, learning their tendencies. Some guys were more aggressive than others. Some were a little more timid and cautious. And some of them, when the door opened, they were gonna take it. Other guys I could bully out of the way. I knew that if I came into the corner and stayed strong and if they ran into me and they hit me, they would be like holy crap—they wouldn't force the issue.

Eliot, the 20-year-old kid from Canada, was wicked fast at the start. But he was younger. Once he got in traffic, his lack of experience showed. He didn't have the same confidence as an experienced rider. So I knew he was going to have a good start. But then, I knew that I could come back and be aggressive against him.

Then you had a guy like Omar Visintin. He was experienced— shoot, he probably had as much experience as me. And he was super fast.

Both of the Italian guys were unpredictable. They were known to take lines that would put them into a corner that they couldn't finish without running into you. Dangerous. I had to keep that in mind.

After all the years, all the heats, so much knowledge had been pumped into my brain. I knew I had to race different people differently. I knew I had to approach every scenario differently.

At times, this sport could be just as mental as it was physical.

When I raced, I went through a long checklist in my mind. Almost instinctually. A series of questions and scenarios: *Where's my opportunity in this race? When can I take it?*

And I'm watching what's going on around me with my competitors. If they're alongside one of the other competitors, I'm studying the situation and tapping into all the experiences in my brain. Replaying experiences. All the heats that I've done. Remembering how this has played out before.

So I started to think, *Okay, these two are up here, that's going to leave me an opening there. Or, if they're going to crash, they're going to crash here. So I need to be able to be ready to go here.*

When you ride the course, you try to find the opportunities. Where can I set myself up? Where can I make a move? But you also have to be flexible. When something changes in front of me, like one of the riders makes a mistake or goes somewhere I didn't expect, I need to be able to take this other line. So you go over strategies for every situation.

But I also knew something else…. I'm faster than these kids, and there ain't no way they are beating me. If you don't have that mentality, you've already lost.

Here we go!

I wore the green vest. Omar was in red, Grodin in blue, and Lorenzo Sommariva in yellow.

Coming out of the start, I settled into second. Through the rollers, off the first jump, I fell into third. But I kept fighting, kept pumping my arms and legs. I was drafting Grondin, who was far ahead. Staying directly behind him, letting him cut the wind, giving me a great advantage.

Drafting was always complicated. But coming out of a draft was so tricky.

If you get out of the draft too early, you just don't get enough speed to finish the pass. So you have to be comfortable, inching closer, basically almost touching their tail. When people go to get out of a draft, you gotta move quick and be decisive. If you get too wide, now you've wasted too much movement, moving laterally rather than going straight forward. And if something doesn't work, if you come out of a draft and can't pass, you have to be able to adjust and get right back in that draft. Right back on that tail.

The whole thing is a crazy mental dance. Making a million decisions in a split second. As you are screaming down a mountain. Coming off jumps. Carving turns. And you have to make adjustments instantly. If you are in a draft and make a big move to get around their board, and you shoot two lanes over, now you've dug that edge into the snow, which slows down your speed. But if you can just stay in there, be calm, and slightly move over and keep that speed, then it will work.

It's an art. For sure.

I slipped into second, going around a couple of big sweeping turns. First right. Then left.

Grodin was in the lead.

But going through the rollers, into the jump section, I stayed in the draft and started to reel him in. With each feature, I got closer and closer. Heading into the jump section, I got within striking distance off the first jump and slipped out of the draft while approaching the second jump. Because of the speed I gained in the draft, I sling-shotted past Grondin going off the jump. I was carrying so much speed that I was able to make a big move and fly the jump way lower that he could. He was twice as high as I was, which was slowing him down, like a kite catching the wind, yanking him back, and that allowed me to slingshot into the lead as we headed into the third corner.

It was like I was supercharged. Zooming into the lead. Holding onto it. Hitting every curve. Staying strong. Not letting anybody pass.

Riding fast.

On the finish line straightaway, I was pumping as hard as I could. Making sure Grondin and Visintin weren't able to pass me. Using everything that I had gained on the pump track around my house during COVID.

Pumping.

Pumping.

Hoping.

Finally, magically, wonderfully, crossing the finish line in first place.

Adrenaline. Relief. Excitement. Joy. Surging through me. Amped up. About to explode.

"YEAH!" I screamed. My patented scream.

I pounded my fist and high-fived Visintin who was close behind me. I got off my board and looked up the mountain. "Let's go, Linds!" I screamed.

The gold medal right there. Within reach. Unbelievable. Chills through my body.

Landon, are you seeing this? Are you seeing all these lessons? Are you seeing what's possible?

I had edged Visintin of Italy by four hundredths of a second. A slim lead. But it was a lead.

And I passed Grondin, a 20-year-old who was half my age. I think he's super talented, has a chance to become the face of the sport, and he's going to be an Olympic champion.

How freakin' sweet. I was an aging athlete, doing a sport that I love, and the younger generation was trying to push me out. And it felt really good to get one more shot and to be able to beat those kids in front of the whole world. And to do it representing Team USA.

What an amazing opportunity

I looked up the mountain and screamed, "Come on, Linds!"

———————

Then, I had to wait. For the most exciting race that I would ever watch.

Lindsey was at the top, rolling her head around, loosening up her neck. The snow was swirling. Not actually coming down; it was going sideways. Swirling around in circles.

The conditions had changed. Again. Didn't bother us. Didn't bother Linds. We've been through this so many times. We've been on every course imaginable. In every condition possible. We knew what to do. She knew what to do.

I had given Linds a slim lead over the Italian team of Omar Visintin and Michela Moioli by 0.04 seconds.

Now it was all up to her. The anchor. The GOAT.

"LET'S GO!" I screamed.

———————

Even though Lindsey's gate dropped first, Italy had the fastest start and took the lead. I stood at the bottom of the hill, screaming encouragement—Olympic gold on the line.

"Get in that draft! Let's go!" I screamed, my voice captured on NBC's broadcast.

On the third feature, Lindsey made a little mistake, and she cycled back to third place. As she gathered her composure and slid in behind the Canadian, I couldn't help but think, *We just won the Olympics.*

Why? Obviously Lindsey is one of the best in the world. She could get out in front and run away from you. But one thing you don't want…you do not want that girl hunting you. Because she's just done it too many times. She knew exactly how to play it. She knew the right strategy. When younger kids get in the draft, they will make mistakes. They won't stay in there long enough. They get scared when they get close. Lindsey isn't afraid of anything. She's a pit bull on course. Fearless. I knew what she'd be thinking at the last second: *I'm getting all the speed that I can from these people. Then when I turn out of the draft, just enough to be able to get alongside and still use that speed, I will be able to pass them.*

Watching Linds, I knew exactly what she was gonna do. *She's gonna draft Michela Moioli, this Italian girl. And she's gonna draft her two jumps, and after she gathers up all that speed, she's gonna pass her.*

That was exactly what she did.

After a series of jumps, Lindsey climbed into second, just as Canada's Meryeta O'Dine and Italy's Caterina Carpano crashed behind her.

I felt bad for those two women who crashed; that was a bummer for them. Fortunately, they were both fine. So all was good. And we were just happy that no one got hurt.

"Come on, girl!" I screamed.

Then, I realized something else. I started thinking about her next move: *She is gonna slingshot up into the draft of the girl in front, and Linds is going to draft her. She's gonna go all the way and then come out of the last corner and pass her, because she's racing a goofy-foot rider.*

In turn four, Lindsey slowed down and stayed behind her.

"Yeah! Come on! Let's get her!" I screamed.

Lindsey looked like she was back at X Games, absorbing the jumps, using the draft whenever she could. She was a pro's pro, comfortable riding close to others, unafraid of the speed.

Watching the GOAT go to work, watching Linds hunt her down, it felt like I was floating outside my body. Like Will Ferrell in *Step Brothers*.

"Use that experience, girl!" I screamed. "Draft her to the finish!"

It was set up perfectly, I thought: *Going into that next corner, knowing that Italian is a goofy-foot rider, she's gonna have to set that corner up more, because she can't turn that turn as tight.*

If you're on your toes, you can take a corner tighter. And Lindsey knew that. Lindsey knew that girl was going to have to open up, so Lindsey went for it. She dived to the inside while the goofy-footed rider had to set up to be able to make the turn. Linds made a tighter turn and cut off a lot of distance traveled. That girl opened up the door, and Lindsey knew that was going to happen. When she's hunting you, you're in trouble.

Suddenly, Linds was in first place. Just like I had expected. Man, it was awesome to watch.

Coming off the final jump, Lindsey subtly grabbed her board, a full-circle moment going all the way back to Torino 2006, basically saying, "Screw you!" to her critics.

She crossed the line first.

GOLD!

WE JUST FREAKIN WON THE GOLD!

Italy's Moioli and partner Omar Visintin, the men's individual SBX bronze medalist, took silver. I ran across the snow and grabbed Linds in a bear hug, wrapping my arms around her neck. I unhooked her board and she kind of fell, both her hands in the air. "Yeah!"

The team from Canada—Grondin and Meryeta O'Dine, the men's and women's silver and bronze medalists—finished third.

We hugged again. "You are so unbelievable," I said. "Way to ride."

I looked at her. "That was beautiful."

Winning by myself would have been great. I would have been very proud of it. But to do it with somebody else, to share that experience with somebody that I had known forever, to be part of something bigger than myself, made it even sweeter.

I leaned over, an entire lifetime of training and disappointment crashing down, a lifetime of dreaming of this moment. My voice was cracking.

"Way to ride!" I screamed. "That was beautiful. You knew when to go for it and when to set it up in the draft."

Reporters would tell me that at 40 years, 57 days, I was the oldest snowboarder to win an Olympic medal. Ever. To beat those kids on the biggest stage felt amazing. To show the world what we can do, what Yoopers can do. No matter how old we are. It doesn't matter where you come from, it doesn't matter how old you are; you can do whatever you want to do!

———————

We did some quick interviews and then went straight to anti-doping to get tested. We packed up all our boards and gear at our wax room at the mountain. After getting everything packed, they brought us back to the village to pack up all our stuff and get ready for more media and the medals ceremony.

Right before the gold medal ceremony, we did a podcast, *In the Village*, with three-time Olympic swimmer Elizabeth Beisel.

"I always try to tell people, we do a sport that's unpredictable," I said. "But because we've done it so many times and we've seen so many things, we can predict a little bit, which gives us a huge advantage and allows an older athlete to still be competitive."

"You know, being an older athlete, like you said, you're also a rad dad," Beisel said. "Can you tell me, you know, what that means? What it's like to be a dad, how stoked you are to go home? And just see your family that's been so supportive throughout this entire journey?"

"Yeah, it's incredible," I said. "To win a gold medal and bring that home…is unbelievable. But that kid, Landon, is the best thing I've ever done and will be the best thing I ever do no matter what. And to be able to show him through my experiences, my actions, what dreaming big and fighting through adversity and never giving up, what can happen when you do that…. So I'm super excited to get back home to let him take that medal to school to just enjoy it and share it with my whole community."

"He is going to have the coolest Bring Your Parents to School Day, show-and-tell type of thing," Beisel said.

"Yeah, it's because I just announced that I will be doing his commencement speech," I said. "I will be doing the commencement speech, and as a dad to be able to do the commencement speech because your son and his friends think you're cool—that doesn't happen that often."

———

More media. More questions.

One question started to come up, almost instantly.

What about the next one? The next Olympics?

In 2026, the Olympics will be held in Italy.

Hmm. I will be 44 at the next Olympics, and my mother is Italian.

Coming off the best season of my career, it made me wonder: *Could I make it four more years? To compete in my mother's native land?* It got me excited, just thinking about it.

———

Yes, we put on the podium outfit. Finally. I had been waiting a lifetime for this moment.

Lindsey and I stood together at the gold medal ceremony, the Olympic rings hanging behind us. We were wearing matching Team USA gear.

"Gold medalists and Olympic champions," the announcer said.

Wow. Just to hear it spoken was stunning.

"United States of America..."

I heard our names and took her hand, helping her step onto the podium. And we both raised our hands in the air. Triumphant.

"If it feels like a fairytale, that's because it is for Lindsey Jacobellis and Nick Baumgartner," the announcer said.

A representative came over holding a platter, like we were being served at a restaurant.

Lindsey took her gold medal and slipped it around her neck—this was her second time on this stage. I took a second to untangle mine and then slipped it over my head.

I shook my head and smiled, punching my fist in the air.

"For Baumgartner, a man who has been on the U.S. Ski Team since 2005, a fourth time at the Olympic Games is a charm. He is finally a medalist, and a gold medalist at that."

Another representative came with a platter of flowers.

Lindsey took one bouquet, I took the other.

"Thank you," I said.

––––––––––––––

I was wearing my Olympic ring.

The one from Vancouver.

The one that symbolized everything for me.

It was scratched and covered in concrete.

In 2018, I returned my Olympic ring to get it remelted, but there was a misunderstanding, and they just cleaned all the concrete out of it and returned it looking semi-new.

But when I took the podium with Lindsey, while getting our gold medals, I was wearing that ring again.

It was covered in concrete again.

Looks so beautiful to me.

And it symbolized everything I had gone through. Just to get to that moment.

––––––––––––––

Lindsey raised her bouquet in the air and I watched her and followed her lead.

Everybody went silent and they played the national anthem.

Lindsey pointed out to me where the flags would rise. She put her right hand on her heart and I, again, followed her lead.

Tears formed in my eyes as I sang along.

Listening to our national anthem. Gold medal around my neck. Singing along. Unbelievable. Just so amazing.

I started to sway back and forth and broke into a smile as it ended.

Lindsey, her blonde hair in tight curls, glanced at me and broke into a giant smile.

We hugged and then put on masks as the other two teams joined us on the podium.

Just amazing.

I was always a huge fan of "The Star-Spangled Banner" and what it stood for. But it hit a little bit different this time.

———————

We didn't get to go to the Closing Ceremony. We went to the village to eat, and they loaded us on a bus for Beijing. We traveled five hours to the airport for a check-in. We flew to Tokyo. Had another five-hour layover. Then to San Francisco, where we had to go through customs. We had to sprint to get to the next flight to Chicago. Once in Chicago, we had another five-hour layover, where I watched the Super Bowl in the Polaris lounge. Then, a 45-minute flight north to Green Bay.

It was like some wild race to get home.

To one of the most magical things I had ever experienced.

PART IV

CHAPTER 14

THE GREATEST PARADE

Traveling back from the Olympics, my phone was blowing up. Half of Iron River was trying to contact me.

"Congratulations!"

"When you gettin' home?"

"We wanna throw a parade."

I called Mike Berutti, my high school football coach and my son's principal at West Iron County High School.

"Coach, I'm coming back to town," I said.

He assumed I meant in a few days.

"Tomorrow."

I was scheduled to fly to Green Bay, Wisconsin—the closest major airport to Iron River—and my sister was supposed to pick me up and bring my truck. She lived just north of Green Bay, and she kept my truck when I was on the road, so it didn't cost a fortune in parking. Berutti called my mom and sponsors and several friends and family, trying to organize something. He offered to hold the event at the high school. "It's the best facility in town," he said. "I'll have the high school ready to go."

Berutti ordered a school bus to carry members of the senior class—basically, my son and his friends—and they started to throw together a parade, which was like piecing together a cardboard puzzle in the middle of a tornado, because it was 3 PM on Super Bowl Sunday and nobody was available. At least, they weren't answering their phones. The Los Angeles Rams were about to beat the Cincinnati Bengals 23–20. Good thing the Green Bay Packers weren't playing, because the entire Upper Peninsula would have shut down. Most Yoopers were Packers fans—none bigger than my dad.

My sponsor KC Atanasoff was a pilot and his company, Krist Oil, had a corporate aircraft. KC considered flying to Green Bay to pick me up, but the plane was down for maintenance.

More than anything, they wanted to control when I would arrive in Iron River. They were afraid that I would arrive at two in the morning, and nobody would be there. Also, they didn't want half the town waiting all day outside in the cold. The Upper Peninsula was in the midst of a bitter cold snap.

They debated where the parade should go and made a parade route from Wisconsin to Iron River, hitting several small towns along the way. But they planned to hold it on February 14—the day after I would arrive. So, they needed to keep me in Green Bay for the night, which was cool with me, because I was exhausted from traveling.

Krist Oil had accounts with several hotels across the region and Atanasoff knew the hotel manager at the Wingate, a hotel across from the Green Bay airport. More importantly, he had that hotel manager's cell phone number. Atanasoff told the hotel manager to keep me at the hotel overnight and that he was going to pay for it.

Then, he found me the coolest ride for the parade—a 45-ton truck. Atanasoff sent me a text message at 7:50 PM on Sunday, February 13, that read: "Here is your chariot! You can ride in it, or on it, it will be there to follow you to make a statement to the Trades. A 45-ton truck on Main Street should draw some attention! So proud of you, Buddy! We'll get everything worked out and firmed up for when you call tomorrow! I stressed that the kids at the school need to be a part of it! And agree with you that around 4 pm will be the best! But I'll keep you posted.... It's going to be so GREAT. So proud of you!"

———————

I landed in Green Bay, got off the plane, and walked toward baggage claim.

"USA! USA!"

I heard the chant before I even had a chance to see anything.

"USA! USA!"

The chant grew louder. Still wearing a mask over my mouth—it was still required in the airports because of COVID—I passed through a security point, the gold medal tucked in my pocket. Olympics theme music blared through speakers in the Green Bay International Airport.

"USA! USA!"

Landon seemed to come out of nowhere, rushing toward me. I grabbed him in a bear hug and squeezed the back of his black hoodie.

"I'm so proud of you," he said.

My heart nearly exploded. Having your son tell you that he's proud of you? What could be better than that? Tears formed in my eyes, and I started to cry, and I thought, *Come on, man. You have cried enough. Hold it together.*

It was overwhelming. I knew some people were going to be at the airport, but I had no idea Landon was going to be there. I saw my sister and hugged her.

"Where's the medal?" somebody screamed.

There must have been 75 people there, maybe more. Friends and family and TV crews. I pulled the medal from my pocket and held it up and everybody screamed. A local TV station asked for a quick interview, and I slipped the medal over my neck and we went outside. "It took 17 years to capture this dream," I said, standing in the cold, outside the airport. "There were a lot of ups and a lot of downs. I'm just glad I didn't quit when things were tough, and we fought through. Look."

I lifted the gold medal and smiled.

"It's just such a good feeling when you put so much work and effort into something and you don't reach that goal—so many times," I said to a different TV crew. "This is a 17-year journey to this, and there's many times I could have given up, and I think a lot of people would have, and I hope that this story shows people that you need to keep fighting."

More tears. I just couldn't keep the emotion down.

I was asked about the emotional NBC interview.

"It's different tears today," I said on camera. "These tears are so much better. It's days like that when you're bummed out and you're disappointed that make days like today so amazing. That's why when you have that adversity, you can't quit. You keep going because the good things are coming."

We went to the Stadium View Bar on Holmgren Way in Green Bay to celebrate. When everybody in the bar realized that I had just returned from the Olympics, a chant spread through the crowd: "USA! USA!"

I don't think I will ever get sick of that. Nothing sweeter than to be an American. I love this country.

"USA!"

It got louder, and it seemed like everybody in the bar was chanting. I walked away from my table, grinning ear to ear, the gold medal dangling from my neck.

"Is that real?" somebody asked, and I walked over to him.

"Yes!" my sister screamed.

"Holy f—k!" the guy said, holding the medal and feeling the weight.

People in the bar whipped out their phones and started taking pictures. Some of me alone, some with them.

"That's unreal, dude."

"Congrats!"

I shook hands and started high-fiving people. It was strange. Those people were so fixated on the end result—the gold medal. Like they had just seen the last few seconds of a movie, and that was satisfying enough. But I don't think they realized the layers of struggle inside that medal.

"Man, you are so lucky," somebody said.

That comment always cracked me up. It seemed like the harder you work, the more sacrifices you made, the luckier, I guess, you could get. Funny how life works like that.

February 14, 2022

The next day was the sweetest Valentine's Day ever.

I got behind the wheel of my black Ford F-150 truck, Landon in the passenger's seat. My sister and her family had painted USA across the back windows.

It was the perfect complement to my personalized Michigan license plate that read NICK B with the Olympic rings to the left side and GO TEAM USA across the bottom.

I looked at the back windows and smiled. Now that was an Olympic chariot. The kind I had waited my entire life to drive.

I'm ready to rock this right on home.

As we started the 140-mile drive from Green Bay to Iron River, my sister took out her phone and started broadcasting on Facebook Live, like she had created her own miniature TV station from the passenger seat of her vehicle, holding up her phone and narrating the action along the route.

She started giving out our location, encouraging everybody to come out and see us along the route. People from around the country started watching her live feed. Liking it. Sharing it. Thumbs-upping it. Leaving the most incredible comments. Emojis floated across the screen.

The first people that I saw were in Pembine, a town of about 1,000 north of Green Bay. They were standing in the parking lot of a church despite the freezing cold weather, a huge sign covering their truck. I almost zoomed by until I saw them out of the corner of my eye, and then at the last minute, I beeped and flipped a U-turn, and went back to see them.

I let them hold the gold medal and take a picture.

"Thank you!" I screamed.

Funny story about Pembine. Years earlier, I was setting up a speaking event at a school in Pembine, and they were gonna give me $200 to come and talk.

"I know some kids will want some autographs," I said. "Can I send you a picture? And can you guys print off a picture for each kid? And I'll make sure I sign one for each kid."

"We'll see."

"I would appreciate it if they were printed off in color," I said. "So that they're a little bit nicer for the kids."

"I don't think we have the budget to be able to do that," they said.

"Well, here's what you're gonna do," I said. "You're gonna take that $200 that you were gonna give me and you're gonna print off color photos for these kids."

I went and gave the talk.

And happily signed color photos for the kids.

———————

We drove north into Niagara—a town of about 1,500—and many of those fine folks were standing in the frigid temperatures, welcoming me home.

We crossed the Menominee River, passing into Michigan. Small clusters of people gathered by the road, screaming as we passed.

Once in Michigan, we were joined by eight police cars, lights flashing. We were given an escort through Iron Mountain—the hometown of Hall of Fame basketball coach Tom Izzo and former NFL coach Stephen Mariucci. Two of the most famous Yoopers ever.

Every year, I tried to attend a golf tournament that raised money for Mariucci's charity, Beacon House. Sort of like a Ronald McDonald House.

Yoopers take care of each other.

Izzo and Mariucci, who were childhood friends, were great guys. Great role models. They had showed me so many lessons over the years, whether they knew it or not: how to handle fame and success with humility, always thinking about others, always trying to help as much as possible, trying to inspire people, especially the kids. They were always proud to represent the Upper Peninsula. Always proud to be Yoopers.

It wasn't like I made a grand statement, but in the back of my mind, I made a promise to myself: *In everything I do, from this point forward, I am going to try to handle this like Izzo and Mariucci. I am going to follow their blueprint. And try to do everything with pure class.*

We followed US-2, which actually crosses back into Wisconsin.

Through Spread Eagle.

Through Florence, a town of 2,319, known for logging and some great hunting and fishing. Then again, maybe that's what this *entire* area is known for.

As we got closer to Iron River, there were more people. More excitement.

Katelyn Tessin, the Krist Oil marketing director, was working to organize everything, and my sister kept broadcasting on Facebook Live.

"Here we go, and we are off again," Ida said.

The comments flowed across Facebook, a string of happiness.

"I have goosebumps—so happy for Nick Baumgartner. So deserving!!!"

"You got lots more waiting at Bates Hall and downtown Iron River."

"Look at the support! Way to go. I'm proud of him."

"Waiting at the library with quite a few people, nice place to stay warm!"

"I am so happy for him I can't stop crying!"

———————————

I looked at Landon. It was so amazing to have him in the truck with me. For him to see this parade, to experience it with me, to hear all the screaming and see the huge smiles and feel all the love; it was one of the greatest things I could have imagined.

He deserved it. He had made so many sacrifices on this crazy journey. Most of the time, people focused on mine. But he had to make sacrifices, too. I've had to leave him for long stretches of time. Too much time. When I went to competitions. Or when I was training. Or when I was pouring concrete. We called each other all the time or saw each other on Facetime. But I know it wasn't the same. It killed me to be away from him. Just broke my heart every time I had to leave him back home. Yes, I got to travel the world. But it was a struggle. It was so difficult on both of us. During the pandemic, when I was home between races, I had to isolate from everybody, isolate from him, to make sure that I wouldn't catch COVID. To make sure I wasn't stuck and prevented from leaving the country.

But to see his smile, sitting in the passenger seat? To hear the pride in his voice? To see how his eyes light up, just experiencing all of this?

Just amazing.

———————

We crossed back into Michigan and everything started to get real crazy. The Florence cops gave way to an insane number of Michigan State police cars, sheriff's deputies, Crystal Falls city workers, Department of Natural Resources vehicles, power company trucks, and road commission vehicles. The first person I saw was Bryan "Chung" LaChapelle, a sports legend and my concrete mentor. He was that guy who always called to see how you're doing when you need a hand with something.

Coming up on Crystal Falls—about 15 miles from my hometown—I felt like the Pied Piper. We were joined by fire trucks, ambulances, yellow dump trucks, and work vehicles with American flags.

It was like a working man's parade. Or like somebody had spilled out my Matchbox cars and lined them up in a row, and they were all following me home.

I had imagined winning an Olympic medal. I had written it down as a goal—when you write out a goal, you have a far greater chance of accomplishing it. And I had envisioned standing on the podium. But this? Beyond my wildest dreams. I guess I had never envisioned the aftermath. The whirlwind.

As we cut through Crystal Falls—a town of about 1,500 people—the crowd got bigger and bigger. People were screaming. We were driving through banners stretched across the road, snapping them in half, like a sprinter hitting the finish line. I saw people that I had grown up with, some of the most amazing people I've ever met in my life.

Sirens were going off. Horns blasting.

I looked in the rearview mirror and saw all kinds of flashing lights. The kind that normally make your heart sink into your stomach and make you think, *Oh man, was I speeding?*

But now, those lights were so cool. So mesmerizing.

As this craziness was unfolding, part of me felt bad for any unsuspecting strangers who were just going about their everyday life, didn't know about any of this, and got stuck behind this circus. Not just in one town, but in town after town.

I felt so lucky, so humbled. None of my teammates had ever gotten a parade like this.

On the southside of Crystal Falls, standing on the sidewalk, I saw Gene Giuliani, one of my brother Josh's best friends, and his entire family. When he was in high school, he had stayed with us often because his house was too far out in the woods. His son was holding an American flag, and he ran alongside the road, chasing us, the flag flapping in the wind

Clusters of people stood in the cold, next to kids and dogs, holding signs and American flags. People in the street were screaming, yelling. That only happened in communities like this. Man, do we have an amazing support system.

I was driving behind two police cars, their lights flashing, sirens blaring. My sister was following me and she was screaming from her truck, "Thank you!" And she kept broadcasting the parade on her Facebook account.

The comments were flowing through Facebook:

"Ida your commentary is the best LOL."

"This is amazing!! NBC 26 keeps going live to the parade."

"What an amazing experience for our children and our community as a whole! Way to go Nick!! We are so proud!!"

"Where are you guys right now?"

And she would tell them. My own personal PR person.

Every few blocks, I saw small clusters of people, maybe a few, maybe a dozen or more—and most were bundled up, bracing against the cold, waving and screaming.

I screamed right back to them: "YEAH! Woo hoo!"

"Thank you!"

Dozens of people. Hundreds of people. It felt like thousands. The longer we went, the more packed it became. It was inspiring and amazing, and I can't thank them enough.

We were all united. I didn't accomplish this. We did. The entire U.P.

As we entered Bates Township, where I grew up, on the outskirts of Iron River, there were people on both sides of US-2, standing in groups. People were honking, holding signs, waving flags.

Somebody posted on Facebook: "Iron River is gonna be rockin.'"

Before the last push to Iron River, we came up on the staging area at a Park-and-Ride lot just down the road from my house. The Crystal Falls vehicles turned off, because the Iron River vehicles were already lined up and ready to finish this parade.

Iron River style.

I got out of the truck and rushed to my mom and dad. They had brought my dog, Oakley, and she sat down next to my legs. I petted her and her tail went crazy, wagging in complete joy. I took Oakley's leash, walked around the parking lot, and started hugging people.

After a few minutes, we loaded back up and started the last segment into Iron River.

Again, I felt like the Pied Piper to a magical parade.

A sign stretched across a giant yellow truck: WELCOME HOME NICK. ONCE A WYKON, ALWAYS A WYKON—a reference to a three-legged creature that is the mascot at West Iron County High School.

We inched forward, passing four ambulances and a school bus with an American flag. Area students were released early from schools, so they could attend the event. Landon had gotten out of my truck and boarded that bus with his classmates. He poked his head out the window and waved, smiling like it was the last day of school before summer vacation. His smile, man; that smile made everything worth it.

Police car lights flashed; fire truck sirens wailed.

My dad was in his Chevy truck, my sister in a vehicle behind him.

I don't know how many trucks and vehicles were behind me. But it had to be more than 30, maybe 50. The final stretch of the parade was a single-file line of fire trucks, police cars, ambulances, Department of Natural Resources vehicles, city work trucks…. Heck, any vehicle they could find. Landon's entire graduating class was in a school bus. It felt like half the Upper Peninsula was in the parade and the other half was standing along the road watching it go by.

Driving down US 2, I screamed out the window, "Yee hee!"

Even the snow was decorated. Somebody had taken blue spray paint and wrote in a snowbank, NICK. MAX EFFORT. And they had finished it with a smiley face.

The parade route toward Iron River was like a trip through my childhood; heck, my entire life. We passed my current house on the right. On the left, we passed Bates School, where I went to elementary school.

We passed my parents' house—you couldn't see it from the road. But it wasn't far off the road. Back through the woods.

As we rolled down the two-lane road, cars pulled over and stopped on the shoulder. Somebody held a sign: NICK'S FROM BATES.

Damn right—and proud of it.

I looked back. Something didn't feel right.

I wanted the Ponsse vehicle to get behind me. Because they deserved it.

Ponsse, a Finnish company that made logging machines, was my longest sponsor. Why in the world would a company out of Finland that builds logging equipment sponsor a snowboarder?

Because I asked, and it just made sense to me, and it made sense for Ponsse, and there were several things that came together just to make it happen. I lived in an area where all my friends were loggers. It was the number one industry in the U.P., so it made sense to go after them. When you tried to find sponsors in the U.P., you had to get creative. So I went after Ponsse with all the determination that I took to snowboarding.

It started with Josh Benson. He was one of my best friends and football buddies from back in the day. I graduated with him, and his dad was one of the first to have a Ponsse machine in the United States and helped with Research & Development.

Lucky for me, because Josh and his dad had a relationship with Pekka Ruuskanen, who was the president of Ponsse North America, and they had told him about me.

Then, we had a chance meeting.

Back when I was racing trucks for this Canadian team that picked me up in 2014, we were racing in Sturgis, South Dakota, during the motorcycle rally, and Pekka always went to that rally race. So he came and checked out the track race. He came up to me and said, "Hey, what's going on? How you doing? I'm Pekka."

"Pekka, I've heard so much about you," I said.

We started talking. Face to face. There was always some talk brewing about a potential sponsorship, but it came together in Sturgis. He agreed to sponsor my snowboarding for the 2014–15 season.

"You should get a group of people and come out to watch the X Games," I said.

So they came out to X Games, and they brought a whole crew. It was crazy…and also quite funny. These guys showed up wearing bright, neon-green safety clothing. Warm winter clothing for working on these machines in the woods. There were 12 to 14 guys in all this safety equipment, and they looked like they were X Games workers.

So, they showed up at X Games in this Sprinter van. It was hard to find parking, hard to do anything. These guys, they were like, *Hey, whatever.* They ended up backing their Sprinter van in with the fire trucks and the police cars. Usually, when you walked into X Games, you had to have a pass and go through security to check your bags. So, we went to the checkpoint, and the security guards looked at the crew in the green safety equipment and said, "No, you guys are good. Go this way."

Because the security people thought they were workers.

These Ponsse guys were having fun, talking shit, playing along: "Oh, yeah, we're with fire and rescue."

I got special passes for them—friends and family passes. I've been at X Games since 2005, so I had a good relationship with these people, and they gave me enough passes for everybody. The only thing it really does is allow you to get a little bit closer to the fence that separates the arena. Rather than being in the third row, the Ponsse guys were now right up front with the family and friends.

Anyone who watched X Games that year on TV saw this huge blob of people wearing safety green in the front row at every event. It looked ridiculous.

One day, we all went to the freestyle snowmobile event. I had to use a bathroom and I asked one of the real security guards, "Where's the closest bathroom?"

The security guard said, "Those fire guys said that they're gonna bring a porta potty up here."

He was looking at my Ponsse crew, the guys in green. And I was laughing inside, as I was thinking, *Those people don't work for you! They don't do anything here!*

"No, they're gonna bring a porta potty up there," the real security guard said. "You'll be good."

It was ridiculous—just hilarious. We took full advantage of what they were wearing. But yeah, they came to X Games and had the time of their lives. I made sure that they had a great time, and Pekka was in my corner ever since, helping to support me to be able to continue to do this. It was so hard, a constant struggle, for me to keep drumming up the sponsors.

It meant a lot for me to have a Ponsse machine in the parade. Josh Benson was in a cab with a bunch of kids. I just wanted them to move the machine right behind me, because Ponsse and the entire Vidgren family (the owners) were so important to me. They deserved it. They had treated me super well—a first-class company. But they treat their customers and their employees exactly the same. When they would throw parties, they made sure that everyone got to come—all the workers and their families and their customers and the customers' families. They made sure everybody would have a blast and party and enjoy themselves. That was how they did things. I always respected them for that. They make sure that everyone feels like part of the family.

The parade just kept rolling. Right through the story of my life.

As we left Bates and entered Iron River, I could see the McDonald's golden arches sign down on the right.

US-2 turned into Adams Street, and we passed the Subway on the left, as well as the AmericInn—all the places where I hung out with friends.

Even though it was cold, it looked like something out of a movie. The sky was crystal blue. There was a blanket of snow on the ground. And in a moment that might only happen in the Upper Peninsula, people rode snowmobiles to the parade and stood by their machines, screaming and cheering.

We passed Krist Oil and the marquee by the road read, WELCOME HOME NICK.

We turned left at the stoplight—the only stoplight in this town; heck, the only stoplight in the entire 1,211-square-mile county. I blew through the red light because a cop was waving us by, turning onto North 4th Avenue.

It was 18 degrees with a frigid wind, but this amazing parade became something even better, something far more magical. Heading into the heart of downtown, the sight was spectacular. I stopped my truck.

"Get somebody to drive my truck," I yelled to my brother. "I'm gonna walk."

There was no way I was going to be waving from the comfort of my warm truck.

I grabbed Oakley, bending down and snuggling her for a picture. Then, I started to walk the route. Horns were going off, sirens blaring.

Countless times I had been on this street, attending more parades than I can remember. But I had never seen so many people in Iron River. I stopped and posed for pictures with anybody who wanted. Some people I didn't even know. But whenever I saw somebody that had played a part in my journey—no matter how big or small—I went up to them and we hugged and I started to cry, tears freezing to my cheek.

"Hey, you guys," I said. "Thank you."

There were high fives and bro hugs and two armed hugs and kisses and smiles and little kids were waving flags.

"Betcha ACE sold outta flags," somebody wrote on Facebook.

My sister was still broadcasting.

People were standing on chairs. Some I hadn't seen in years.

"Oh, my God!"

"Congratulations!"

"So proud of you."

"You made us so proud!"

"Thank you!'

I walked down Genesee Street, holding Oakley's leash in my left hand, her tail wagging, while pumping my right fist.

Or wiping tears from my eyes.

I spotted my older brother Robby, who was my hero growing up.

"This is amazing," I said.

He was six years older than me and I modelled everything after him—I played football, wrestled, and ran track, just like Robby. And I tried to work my ass off, just like Robby.

"I've never seen anything like it," he said. "You deserve every bit of it."

Which only made me cry again.

Friends and relatives and people from all over the Midwest lined the sidewalk, spilling into the street. How did they all get here? How did they even know? Just from my sister's Facebook?

Most were holding flags.

"Congrats, Nick."

It was wall-to-wall people.

More horns and sirens. My sister was still taking a Facebook live video and people jumped out from the sidewalk, taking video of her. A video of a video. Like some crazy surreal dream.

All those years, all those disappointments, all the trips and late-night drives and planes and hotels and condos and European break-fasts and time away from Landon—all of it was crashing down on me. Or maybe it was helium now, and it was lifting me off the ground.

The crowd kept growing. Everybody stood shoulder to shoulder. Two deep, three deep. Hundreds of people, maybe more than that. Music was blaring. It was crazy. People I didn't even know were screaming and yelling, spilling out of their businesses, lining the road.

Past River North Pub.

Past the local library.

Past City Hall.

Past Outer Limits Bar and Grill.

Heading toward the high school. Most of the people in Iron River work for the school system or the hospital. We had a bowling alley until about 10 years ago. But someone broke in the theater, and they never replaced the projector.

But no one focused on what we didn't have.

Because what we *did* have was amazing.

Like Riverside Pizzeria.

I had been all over the world, and Riverside was the best pizza joint in America. Heck, the best pizza on the planet. There was no close second. Yeah, sure, I've eaten at some fine Italian pizza places in the world. Mainly in Italy. I'd give you that. Some places had some good stuff, but I love what I grew up with. And Riverside will always be my favorite pizza.

Some kids had rosy cheeks—I had no idea how long they had been in the cold, because we were late. Nobody could have antic-ipated how big this parade would be. We turned right to head up Stambaugh Hill. I jumped in the back of the truck because there were just a few people standing on the steep hill. But at the top of the hill, I jumped out of the truck again, because the crowd grew. I walked down the hill, hugging people, high-fiving, posing for pictures, and we made the final half-mile walk to the Charles Greenlund Gymnasium. The crazy thing about that—Coach Chuck Greenlund was not only my dad's football coach but also my football coach my sophomore and junior years.

Inside the gym, they didn't know if 30 people would show up.

But there were close to 1,000—unbelievable.

What a magical moment.

Suddenly my old football coach realized they had forgotten only one thing—a recording of the national anthem. As my old coach scrambled to find some music, the high school orchestra teacher got up and lead the crowd, everybody singing together. A cappella. All these voices lifting up, rocking the gym, so much better than a recording ever could have been.

The lights dimmed and they introduced me. I walked into the gym, a spotlight hitting me, getting treated like some freakin' rock star, arm in arm with Landon, holding Oakley's leash, all of us walking out together. A dad, a son, and his dog.

I pumped my fist and everybody was clapping.

I spotted Grandma B, my 95-year-old grandmother on my dad's side. She was always a special person in our lives. My grandfather on my mom's side had passed away years ago, before I ever made it to any Olympics. He was a Golden Gloves boxer. He was into sports and I wish that he could have seen me in the Olympics. For him to know that I went to the Olympics would have been very cool. But Grandma B had been able to see my entire career. And for her to be in this gymnasium, for her to hear these screams, it was so amazing.

U.S. Rep. Jack Bergman of Watersmeet stood at the far end of the gym, and he spoke first: "Ladies and gentlemen, what an honor for all of us to be here today to celebrate something so positive."

Everybody clapped and whistled.

"So much so, that we collectively, I believe, took that run with you, Nick," Bergman said.

Everybody laughed.

"We did not have the intestinal fortitude to do what you did," Bergman said. "But we are glad you did. Because what you showed, over a long period of time, is what we in the United States of America are known for. Number one, pride in who we are. Number two, passion for what we do. Three, the persistence to carry on when times get tough. But the ability to see past the times when we may fall, the times when it's tough to get up. Because we have our goal in mind. And you did it, you did it, the two of you, you did it individually. I'm so proud of you. And I say that for the entire House of Representatives, I'll let them know when I get back to Washington, D.C."

He stood with his back to the West Iron County scoreboard, and everybody clapped.

"God love you, God bless you, and bless you for being you," Bergman said.

"Yeah!" my sister screamed, still recording everything on Facebook.

Bergman marched across the floor and I gave him a hug. We posed for a picture, and I held up the gold medal.

So much of my life was in this gym. Not just the people, but everything on the walls.

Up on the far wall, there was a banner for the Wykon wrestling team. Under "100 Wins," my name was listed second, for winning 122 matches from 1997 to 2000. Under the heading "Undefeated

Seasons," I was one of four people named because I went 37–0 in 1998.

There were 14 wrestlers listed for being U.P. Champions. My brother Beau won championships in 1997 and '98, and I was listed for winning a title in 2000.

In the corner of the gym, there was a record board for the track team. I still held the school record in the 110-meter high hurdles at 15.26 seconds in 2000.

There were people from all over the Upper Peninsula—coaches and athletes and people I had met just once, after giving a speech at their high school.

Amazing. I walked to the podium with the gold medal around my neck, a baseball cap on my head—some of the Olympic swag. I pumped my right hand, and my left hand was stuck in my pocket.

"USA!" everybody chanted. "USA!"

Red, white, and blue balloons were scattered across the basketball court. A United States flag was set up to my right, an Olympic flag to my left. A poster with the Olympic rings was on the wall behind me.

"All right, well, we'll give this a try," I said.

Everybody laughed and I adjusted the cap on my head, trying to stay composed.

"Ah, thank you guys so much," I said. "It means so much for me to be able to bring this home for you guys."

I pulled the medal away from my chest and looked down at it. I felt so much love and support from the entire area. There's nothing like representing your country, your family, your community.

I hoped that medal would bring respect to the entire Upper Peninsula. Respect that it deserved.

I hoped that medal would show people how tough we are and how hard we are willing to work to get what we want.

"I know you saw my interview after the first event," I said. "Obviously, I was emotional and bummed out. But I'm glad you got to see it because"—and here I shrugged—"that's what we do. We go out there, we give it everything we've got. We put everything on the line chasing greatness. And sometimes we fall short."

Everybody who meant something to me in the world—at least almost everybody—was in that gym.

"That one hurt bad for me because, mainly, I'm running out of chances."

Light laughter rolled through the crowd.

"I'm getting older," I said. "I guess I didn't know at that point I was 100 percent sure that I was going to be able to compete in the mixed-team event. I mean, I probably should have known. If I would have paid attention, I probably would have."

Everybody laughed.

"We had two teams," I said. "I wasn't sure, at the moment, when I went through the mixed zone and did my interviews. Afterward, I took 20 minutes. I cried a lot. I tried to gather myself and I finally said, 'OK, let's do this interview.'

"Then, she started to talk and I cried some more."

There was more laughter—Yoopers don't take themselves too seriously.

"The one thing—I used the word letdown, and you guys, I didn't let you down at all," I said. "I do appreciate all the messages that I got from you guys, to build me back up again. I know the people who truly cared and are behind me would never be disappointed."

The gym went quiet. "I'm so glad that I got a shot at redemption, two days later," I said. "So glad."

A baby started to cry.

"Once I knew we had two teams, I immediately knew that I'd be partnering with Lindsey Jacobellis," I said.

Somebody screamed: "Yeah!"

"I know everybody was asking, 'How did they make that team, how did they do it?'"

"Our coaches sat down and had a meeting and tried to figure out what would be the best team to get a medal. On Team USA, we want to win medals and bring them home. Because we are competitive. We want to show the world that we are the best. So I knew right away because of our experience and our age"—I shrugged and heard people laughing—"that Lindsey and I would be competitive together. She had been on the team for 20 years and I've been on the team for 17, which is crazy. So over the course of time you build a relationship and a bond with somebody, and my sport is so unpredictable—you guys, anything can happen. We've been there long enough and have seen enough things happen that we can predict the unpredictable. But to go up there and get another shot, a chance at redemption. For me, at that moment, it wasn't really—don't get me wrong, I wanted a medal—but it wasn't really about this."

I held up the gold.

"It was about, I wanted to show everyone. I had something to prove. I wanted to show that if I didn't make that one little mistake, I could have won that individual race. And I wanted my performance to show that."

The baby kept crying.

"What's so cool about the team event...there is so much pressure that comes with the Olympics in any sport. With the individual race, it's so on you. But when you have the team event, with another rider, you know you can make one little mistake because the absolute best female snowboarder of all time is going to back you up."

Everybody broke into applause.

"So for me, the team event is more fun," I said. "I go in smiling and having fun and enjoying myself. I learned a long time ago that when I'm smiling, having fun and not so worried about winning and not putting so much pressure on myself, I rise to a whole different level. I was very, very proud to be able to share that with the world and show them what a Wykon can do."

More applause.

"You guys saw me cheer for her," I said. "That's how you cheer for a teammate. That's how you root on a team, and I know that's how you guys cheered me on. I can't even imagine the crazy things you guys were doing in front of your TVs. I'm sure you looked crazier than me and I appreciate that very much. A question that I've been getting a lot: What do you hope this gold medal does? For me, I just hope people see what's possible. Seventeen years—"

I started to break down with emotion, and everybody started whistling and screaming and clapping.

"Seventeen years," I said. "I gave it everything I had. Every year, it takes more and more and more. I know everyone says they knew I could do it.'"

I smiled.

"There were a lot of you who didn't think I could do it," I said. "I don't blame you—40 years old, I didn't get it done when I was in my prime. And now here we are at 40, and I don't blame you."

Everybody laughed.

"But rather than listen to that, I used it to inspire me. I've never sacrificed or worked as hard as I did in this offseason. I did that for a reason. I know I'm running out of chances. I wanted so bad to bring this back to the people who have been behind me and supporting me."

I lifted up the medal and laughed.

"You guys, we did it," I said.

Everybody started screaming.

"We did it and it felt so good," I said. "Coming from the U.P., everybody says we have a lot less opportunities. And they are not wrong. I could have made excuses. I could have said that I don't know any professional snowboarders. I didn't have any sponsors when I started. How can I do this? I could have settled and let it be that. But I hope you guys see that I did everything that I could…. You guys, maybe it's not snowboarding, maybe it's not sports, but find what you are passionate about. Find what you love. They say if you find what you love, you won't work a day in your life. But I don't believe that."

Everybody laughed.

"You work harder than you ever imagined, but you love every minute of it," I said. "Seek out what you are passionate about. You got one shot at life. Do what you love. It doesn't matter if you are getting older. At 40 years old, I went to the Olympics and won a gold medal."

People in the crowd started screaming.

"It's important to live life on your own terms," I said. "And have as much fun as you can."

I let out a sigh.

"Ah, I just hope this story shows you it's possible," I said.

More applause, more whistling.

"To my family, my friends, everyone—and I know a lot of people wrote messages, but I haven't written back because—ah, there's a lot of them."

More laughter.

"I had more than 1,000 text messages on my phone," I said. "I've gone through about half my Instagram messages, and I haven't even touched my Facebook messages. So you guys, it's not that I'm too cool now that I have a gold medal. But it's just going to take some time. I'm going to read every single one of those messages because that's what has helped me get through the tough times and work through the adversity... Once a Wykon, always a Wykon."

I lifted up the medal and everybody started screaming again.

"Way to go Nick!" somebody screamed.

"We love you!" somebody else screamed.

———————

When I got home, my son looked at my medal and said, "I have to know if it's real. I have to know what it's worth."

So, he looked it up.

Turns out an Olympic gold medal is $500 worth of silver wrapped by $400 of gold.

I do like silver, especially when it's covered in gold.

I did a pep assembly at the same gym the next day, so all the kids could attend. Then I did another on the other side of the county in Crystal Falls.

A few days later, I went to the U.P. 200 Sled Dog race in Marquette. Hundreds of people showed up, even though it was bitterly cold.

They asked me to give a speech before the 228-mile race from Marquette to Grand Marais and then back. Nothing quite said Yooper pride than watching thirteen 12-dog teams in an Iditarod qualifier. But there were other races, like an 82-mile race to Chatham and back, and the Jack Pine 30, a 23-mile race featuring six-dog sled teams.

Dogs and Yoopers. The essence of life.

"When people ask me what a Yooper is, I can't explain it in words," I told the crowd. "You have to come up here, you have to meet us to understand what we are. I couldn't be more proud to be from somewhere. We brought a gold medal to the Upper Peninsula of Michigan, where it deserves to be."

It was wild. For two years, I practically hid from the world, trying to make sure I didn't get COVID. I stayed away from my family. In isolation. I didn't go anywhere, just to make sure that I didn't get sick and that I could travel to training camps and competitions.

But after five days back in the Upper Peninsula, I got it right away. I tested positive for COVID.

Maybe that was a blessing in disguise. I had been running on little sleep, just adrenaline since winning the gold. And there were no signs of any letup or of getting any sleep any time soon. So COVID forced me to just relax, decompress a little bit, enjoy some time at home. And it was super nice.

I considered it a brief pause. A short rest.

Because the plans started running through my head:

I want to visit as many schools across the Upper Peninsula as possible. And we're going to do that until the end of the school year. Plus, I'll be coaching track and field for Landon. I'm gonna go, go, go.

I got an email saying, "*MTV Cribs* wants to come to your house."

And I was like, *You gotta be freakin' kidding me. This is insane.*

I grew up on MTV. Every morning, I would turn on music videos and get ready for school while Beau was kicking my ass.

But *MTV Cribs* was always cool—I watched it all the time. You'd see all these celebrities with monster houses and I was like, *OK, my house is nothing like what you have ever seen on the show. You sure they want it?*

They said, "Heck yeah."

They loved that I built the house with my brothers and my friends, they loved my snowboard pump track that I built around my house in the winter, and they loved the story behind my van.

So I was like, *Oh, OK. Sweet.*

And an entire crew came to shoot some video.

I thought the episode turned out pretty cool. More than anything, I'm proud because they showed so much of Iron River. It was like a giant postcard from my hometown. Or a tourist video. The show started out with some images from across town, setting the scene. They showed the Iron River water tower, as well as the Iron River Family Foods—our grocery store—with a sign out front that read: WAY TO GO BUMMIE OLYMPIC GOLD 1ST U.P. MEDAL IN 62 YEARS.

They used a drone to shoot some cool video and zoomed in on my van, setting up a joke to start the show.

The screen said: NICK'S CRIB, 2 FRONT SEATS, 1 MATTRESS, 16 SQUARE FEET, ACTIVITY AREA.

I swung the van door open: "What's up, MTV?" I said, crouched in the back. "I'm Nick Baumgartner and welcome to my crib."

They showed my front seat and flashed to the passenger seat. Zooming in on the back of my van. I had put the mattress in it—the same one that I had used the previous summer when I was camping and training at AdvantEdge in Marquette.

"All right guys, this is where I sleep," I said, playing along. "This is my nice little bed."

It was only half a fib. I actually did sleep in that van. Oakley was sitting up on the bed—I love that she was on MTV.

"My dog, Oakley, keeps me company," I said.

"I'm just kidding. This isn't my real house."

"Let's go check out my real home."

The screen flashed the real info about my house:

NICK'S CRIB

4 BEDROOMS

2 BATHROOMS

1,540 SQUARE FEET

SNOWBOARD TRACK

I stood out front. "All right, guys; welcome to my actual home."

I was wearing a long-sleeved T-shirt that read, NEVER UNDER-ESTIMATE AN OLD MAN WITH A SNOWBOARD.

They flashed through several scenes inside my house. "I bought this house in 2008," I said. "And I've since doubled the footprint. Let's go in the house and see if it's a little nicer than that van I have."

OK, so I didn't tell them everything about my house. In spring 2008, I got a call from my friends: "Hey, dude, they are selling the house right next door."

"Oh, really?" I said.

Two of my childhood best friends were next-door neighbors: Mike, who lived across the street, and his sister Katie and her husband, who is also a good friend.

They were all like, "Yeah, dude, come get it."

So, we went over and made an offer and then bought the house

"All right, welcome," I said on the show. "This is the inside of my home. I hope you like this a little bit better."

I bought this house for $19,000, and I think the down payment was $1,500 or something. I lived in it, and it was kind of just outdated—kind of a shithole for a long time. And then I decided to take the plunge. When the snow melted, I got my uncle to come down there. My fake uncle, my dad's best friend, Uncle Goober. He came down and dug out the basement—or most of the basement—with his backhoe. He just dug a huge hole next to my house and I put a basement the same size right alongside it. Guess it helps when you are a concrete guy.

The MTV cameras zoomed all around the room, revealing my family, sitting at the counter.

"This is my son, Landon," I said.

Landon wore a blue sweatshirt. "My mom, Mary," I said, pointing at her. "My dad, Robert. He goes by Bone. If I do anything in here you don't like, you can't blame me; you gotta blame the parents."

I smiled. It was an inside joke for Bryan "Chung" LaChapelle. Because he always said that.

"These countertops I actually poured myself," I said, as the cameras zoomed in on the concrete countertops in the kitchen. "People think I'm a professional snowboarder and make good money. But it's actually my concrete work and my manual labor that pays for my dream."

I was dang proud of those countertops. "Came out beautiful," I said.

The camera zoomed in on my refrigerator. "We know you guys love to see the fridge, so let's see what I got here in mine," I opened the door.

The top row: White Claws.

My guilty pleasure.

I pulled out some pizza from my favorite pizza place.

"Riverside Pizza from here," I said. "I've been to 20 countries all over the world. Still the best pizza I've had."

I was being honest. The best.

"And these things, right here," I said, pulling out a white paper bag. "This is what Yoopers eat. This is called a pasty. This is meat and potatoes, veggies, all rolled into one ball."

This was my favorite part.

I loved showing MTV what Yoopers are all about. I pulled my dad into the frame. He wore a grey T-shirt that read, YOOPER 7 COURSE MEAL. PASTY AND A SIX PACK.

"Yoopers are the natives who live in the Upper Peninsula," I said. "It's actually a real word. Webster's put it into their dictionary a few years back. So, it was a proud moment for us Yoopers. [But] Apple still doesn't recognize it as a real word. We gotta get that fixed soon."

We moved into the living room. My gold medal was in a case, under the TV.

"Here's my Olympic medal," I said. "Unbelievable. Dreaming about it is one thing. Holding it in your hand and having it on your mantel is another. Wow, is that a cool feeling."

They took pictures from around town.

Of the giant billboard on the edge of town with my picture.

"None of my friends went home to these parades," I said.

The racing bibs from my four Olympics and one from the X Games in which I won gold were on the wall.

"This is my son Landon's room," I said. "I think the next thing to do is check out the secret room."

We climbed a ladder built into the closet, which lead to a secret, second-floor hideout.

"Yeah, how cool is this?" I said. "I wanted him to have his own space."

Then, we went into my bedroom.

"Right here, my bedroom, where all the magic happens," I joked. "Or doesn't happen, I don't even know." I couldn't hang out with people during COVID.

They showed the closet that I turned into a bathroom. But to be honest, I had just partially finished it. And the toilet wasn't even fastened yet. The magic of TV

"A week ago, this place was a walk-in closet," I said.

I put a TEAM USA PARKING ONLY sign above the toilet.

"Park here, have a little time to yourself," I joked.

The show ended with me on the snowboard track I built around my home.

I had built it before going to the Olympics. It gave me a place to train and it was an amazing workout, but the main reason that I spent 30 hours building a track was because it made me feel like a kid again. An eight-year-old building a snow fort, smiling and having fun. COVID was insanely tough on everybody, and the pressure of the Olympics was building, so I used it as therapy. It was hard to stay upset when you went outside and played in the snow, acting like a kid, building a fort.

"All right, MTV," I said. "Thanks for coming. I appreciate you guys making the trip up here to the Upper Peninsula to check out my home, my track, and my van. But it's time to go. I gotta get back to training."

I flipped on my goggles and went down the small hill. I pumped through some rollers, took a jump onto the roof of my van, and curved around the front of my house.

It made for some great TV.

Home sweet home.

CHAPTER 15

SHARING THE GOLD

M Y LIFE TURNED into a wild whirlwind, and I tried to share that gold medal with everybody, hoping it would inspire somebody.

I went to the White House and took pictures with President Joe Biden, the third sitting U.S. president I've met. Almost immediately, I got a bunch of nasty messages from lots of people. It was amazing how many people saw that picture and decided to spread a bunch of hate. There was a lot of stuff that I disagreed with in politics, but I respected the Office of the President and I don't care who was sitting in that chair—I would not turn down the chance to go to the White House to meet them. It doesn't mean I agree with everything they say. It kills me to see all the hate that people decided to write about me in the comments and my inbox. I don't care what they say about me, but it sucks that this is where we are in society. I had people saying the high gas prices were my fault; that I was a disgrace to my hometown; that I was a disgrace to the U.P.—all because I got to meet the president and he was nice to all of us.

There is just too much hate in the world.

I hope that my journey and how I am sharing this medal with everyone and taking time to be kind to everyone can help inspire people to be nice to one another regardless of their different opinions.

Gandhi said it best: "Be the change you want to see in the world."

───────────────

I carried the gold medal in my pocket as I toured Michigan State with Landon. He was planning to go there for college. I texted Tom Izzo, the legendary MSU coach: "Hey, we are here."

But at first, he didn't text me back.

"Maybe he's mad because I'm stealing some of his Yooper thunder," I joked with Landon.

Izzo was born in Iron Mountain, about 45 minutes from Iron River. He is best friends with Steve Mariucci, a former NFL coach. Every year, I tried to attend a charity event that raised money for the Steve Mariucci Family Beacon House in Marquette. It has 20 private guest rooms, two overnight support suites, a community kitchen, and a chapel.

What an amazing place. If you have a loved one who is sick, you can stay at the Beacon House, and it makes it a little bit easier.

One year, I donated my entire Olympic outfit to raise money for the Beacon House.

I met Izzo at the charity event, so I have his number, and I called him, but he wasn't able to answer.

But finally, we got in touch and Landon and I headed over to his office.

One of Izzo's assistants gave us a tour of the basketball facility, and I saw his championship rings and trophies.

Izzo came in and looked at me. "It used to be me and Mariucci. Now this guy is doing it."

"It's funny you say that," I said. "I just told that to the kids. I said, 'I hope Izzo is not getting mad.' I'm not trying to steal some of your Yooper game."

As he was shaking Landon's hand, Izzo looked at me and gave me a little nod. Then he came up and gave me a hug.

"We were watching your race right here," Izzo said, gesturing at a TV in his office. "All of my coaching staff was like, 'Oh, yeah.' I can't remember where Mariucci was, but he couldn't watch it. So there I am. I was videotaping it on my phone so that I could send it to Mariucci."

I was kind of floored. To have Coach Izzo, this legend from the Upper Peninsula, filming my race so that he could send it to Coach Mariucci, another Yooper legend, was pretty cool. It was even cooler just because I'm a Yooper and I grew up knowing those guys as legends. They both had a huge influence on me. As I got more attention, I tried to handle it just like they had, by giving back and acting the right way.

We started taking pictures, and Izzo said, "I gotta put this thing on." He slipped the gold medal over his head, and he was giggling like a kid in a candy store. That floored me even more. Here was Coach Izzo, a guy who has had so much success as a basketball coach, and he was just giggling.

It was pretty awesome, a great feeling.

Then, I saw a cardboard cutout of Mariucci.

"Oh, man; come on, Izzo, we got to get a picture with this and send it to Mooch," I said, referring to his nickname.

We took a picture and I posted it on social media.

Landon and I headed to the spring football game, and we were treated like royalty. We toured the football locker room and were taken onto the field. I did interviews with the Big Ten Network and the MSU radio network. As we walked along the sideline, so close to the action that I heard the pads popping and it felt like I was back at Northern Michigan, people leaned over the railing, asking for pictures. Some of them were Yoopers—so and so knew so and so—and I swear the U.P. was just one giant neighborhood. Everybody knew everybody. Everybody was tied together…somehow.

I walked around with the gold medal in my pocket and pulled it out anytime anybody wanted, posing for countless pictures.

I just hoped it inspired somebody.

May 22, 2022
Chicago, Illinois

At a fundraising event in a fancy ballroom in Chicago, I stood next to Michael Phelps, the Olympic swimmer. I held the gold medal in my hand.

"I've got the one thing Michael Phelps doesn't have," I teased. "A gold medal from the Winter Olympics!"

Everybody laughed.

But then I got serious.

"I had a dream a long time ago," I told the crowd. "I put 17 years of my life into a goal. To win that gold medal. I don't come from money, and it was a very tough road for me."

This was a fundraising event for Phelps' charity. A charity that had actually helped me at one point. Years ago, Phelps' charity—along with the Ross Powers Foundation—gave me $3,500 to help offset my training costs.

"After 17 years of falling short of my dream," I said, choking up with emotion.

Phelps took over for me.

"There aren't many 40-year-old Olympians," Phelps said, looking at me. "Especially gold medalists!"

The crowd erupted in cheers.

"I'm from a small town in the middle of nowhere in the Upper Peninsula, Michigan," I said. "I put 17 years of my life into a goal to achieve that gold medal and it's rooms like this that have made it possible."

"I don't come from money," I said. "And it was a very tough road for me. But it was organizations like this, people like you, that made this dream possible."

I pulled out the gold medal.

"We can't do this alone," I said. "We need you guys. So let's have some fun, let's raise some money."

CHAPTER 16

INSPIRING KIDS

FOR SEVERAL MONTHS after winning the gold medal, I crisscrossed Michigan to Wisconsin, giving 53 speeches. Most of them were at Upper Peninsula schools, but some were at libraries or nursing homes—all over. The farthest that I traveled by car was to a library in Pentwater, a small town on Lake Michigan in the Lower Peninsula, which was 445 miles from Iron River and took about seven and a half hours.

I wanted to reach as many students as possible, because the children from the U.P. needed a jolt of hope and inspiration.

So much had changed. When my parents were growing up in Iron River, there were thriving stores throughout town. On Friday nights, everybody went to town early, got a parking spot, and they all just sat there and walked up and down the street. But the mines closed, people moved out, schools became smaller, and businesses closed.

So, these children needed to know anything was possible, if they would only set a goal and go for it. And I felt compelled to share that message with them.

More than anything, I wanted my story to inspire the kids, to give them hope. To teach them if they wanted something, if they worked hard enough, they could accomplish anything in life.

Krist Oil, my sponsor, was so cool—they paid for my gas to drive to all these schools, giving me gas cards. KC saw it as a way to inspire future employers and improve the U.P. What's good for the U.P., he always said, is good for Krist Oil.

At each stop, I made sure I had time to take pictures with the kids. Because I know kids this age; they like to have pictures to post on social media. That was a big part of it. So I wanted to be able to give them what they wanted.

Every stop was different. Sometimes I spoke in a gym. Sometimes I spoke in an auditorium. But I tried to give them one central message: *We are Yoopers. We come from a small town with fewer opportunities, and we have to work a little bit harder. Nothing is ever given to us and nothing is ever easy. We go out and we fight for our opportunities. It doesn't matter where you come from. And it doesn't matter how old you are. As long as you don't give up on your dreams, anything is possible. And when you have setbacks, you have to fight through that adversity. Really, anything is possible.*

I had given speeches throughout my career. I wasn't good at first. You're gonna suck at something at first, but just keep doing it. You get better every time. And this felt different. Now that I had a medal, the kids became more engaged. Their jaws were on the floor, and they were just blown away. They were listening to everything that I said so attentively, almost like they were putty in my hands. It was so different. Before, people were interested and wanted to hear what I had to say. But not to the extent that they were after the gold medal. The change was incredible.

While I told my story, I tried to sprinkle in some advice, the lessons that they could find from my journey. I love being from the U.P. I love being a Yooper. But I encouraged these kids to experience life outside of the U.P. *The Upper Peninsula is an amazing community. But it's kind of a bubble, right? There's a lot more to this world and I urge you to go out and see some of it, whether that means going to Wisconsin or father away. It doesn't have to be surfing in Fiji on the other side of the world. But there's so much to see in this world, and try to see as much as you can. You got time. Go see this world. I've seen some of the craziest, coolest, most awesome views in the world. Like the top of the mountain in Switzerland. It makes you feel so small, but it is one of the most amazing experiences I've ever had. For powder, deep powder, Japan is the best. Fiji is probably the coolest place I ever went. When we would travel back from New Zealand, it's just a two-hour flight to Fiji, and it doesn't cost any more to have your flight stop there. So I got to do two surf trips in Fiji, which was unbelievable. You grow so much when you visit other places, and I encourage you to do it as much as possible.*

I encouraged them to take care of their bodies: *This vehicle right here, this body is gonna take you to the end. When you get older, everything changes. So take care of it. Keep your health, do everything you can to stay as fit as possible, just so you can continue to have fun. And if you get injuries along the way, work hard on your physical therapy to strengthen everything. I am 40 years old. If you look at everything I've been through, all the pain and injuries, I shouldn't be walking around, let alone winning a gold medal at the Olympics. I broke my back. Six weeks before the last Olympics, I got 15 screws and a plate in my shoulder, and I won the X Games 12 days after. So bad things can happen. But with hard work, you can get over it. I promise you.*

I encouraged them to face their fears: *Don't be afraid. Try as many things as you can. Keep throwing darts at the dartboard until one of them sticks. Until you find what you truly love. And I know it's terrifying sometimes to try something new, because you don't want to be terrible at something. But you can't let that fear hold you back. Because I'm telling you, when you do find what you love, you're going to be very glad that you were able to fight through that fear and try it.*

I encouraged them to get involved with sports: *Sports taught me about teamwork and working hard and cheering for my teammates. The lessons you learn in sports, of failure, fighting through adversity, you will need those lessons in every part of life. Because things are not always going to go your way. There's gonna be so many speed bumps along the way, but it's important that you learn how to deal with that.*

I encouraged them to embrace their emotions, not to be afraid of nervousness, but to use it: *Nerves are a big thing, not just in sports but in life. We can't be afraid of nerves. I love to feel that energy. That's the feeling that I'm chasing, getting in that gate, terrified of what's going to happen. And there are so many questions that go with it: Can I make this happen? Is everything good? And the only thing I can tell you guys about nerves and how to control them is preparation. If you are prepared, and you've done everything in your power to be ready for what you're about to do, that is the only way to control those nerves.*

And I hoped it would light a fire under their butts: *Sometimes, you need a little bit of fire and a little push to say, 'Hey, you guys got this.' Because when you're young, I think you overthink things and you're too afraid to fail and to try new things.*

I hoped it would inspire these kids from different cultures: *Snowboarding took me around the world and introduced me to all kinds of different cultures. I love America. But it is so cool to meet people with similar stories from different areas. Maybe they have different challenges. Sometimes, through sports, we can shed a different light on problems. Sometimes our government doesn't get things right. So we can come together through sports. I hope to inspire kids from the USA to be kind and work hard for what they want, to be part of the solution, not the problem. It's truly an honor to be able to inspire good things rather than hate and war.*

I encouraged them to believe in themselves: *You guys are so capable of doing crazy things. You are the perfect age. You can pick whatever you want to do; You can fail at it; and then you can pick another thing. And you can fail at that and pick another thing and you're still young. Just go out there and don't sell yourself short.*

I encouraged them never to set limits on themselves: *Don't ever let someone say, well, you're pretty good for someone from the U.P. Because it's not true. Come on. I hate that. That's one thing as an athlete, we always hear, "Well, you're good at football, for being from the U.P." No! We're tougher. We have to work a little bit harder. But in the long run that definitely builds us up and sets us up for success. As long as we don't give up on ourselves. As long as we stay on the good track. Don't get sidetracked. Don't get into trouble. Because life is way too fun to be held back and not be allowed to have some fun.*

July 4, 2022
Ishpeming, Michigan

I was asked to be the grand marshal of the July 4 parade in Ishpeming, a small town about one and a half hours to the northeast of Iron River. It felt so fitting because Ispheming is considered the home of organized skiing. The National Ski Association was organized in Ishpeming in February 1905. It was later renamed the U.S. Ski Association, which became the U.S. Ski and Snowboard Association.

So, when they asked if I would attend the parade, I said, "Oh, hell yeah."

I hopped on a podcast with Justin Koski, the executive director of the U.S. Ski and Snowboard Hall of Fame.

"Today's about the Fourth and celebrating Nick, who grew up just about an hour and a half away," Koski said on the podcast. "We call him a Super Yooper, and he's joining the ranks of a few other Super Yoopers here coming back with the gold."

A "Super Yooper?"

I had to disagree. I didn't feel like I did anything special. All I did was not give up. I refused to quit when times got tough. I got knocked down over and over again but I always got up. That's the key to success. That was all I did.

If you ask me, Izzo and Mariucci are true Super Yoopers. There is still a lot of good that I need to do for the communities and the people of the Upper Peninsula before anybody could put me up in that kind of territory.

"You can't script stories like this," I said on the podcast. "I'm telling you, that's the beautiful thing about being part of the Olympics is the stories that you hear of people overcoming adversity and winning. These stories are nothing short of unbelievable."

We were joined on the podcast by Seth Wescott, one of my close friends, who is now an NBC announcer.

"It was really kind of fun, just the lead-in throughout the winter following these guys and, you know, messaging back and forth with Baum a bit, and the same with Lindsey," Wescott said. "Lindsey had gotten hurt in the fall, broke her elbow in a skateboarding accident. So seeing her trajectory, coming into the Games and how her time trial results were getting faster, and Nick had gone out and secured his spot early in the World Cup season with a couple of great results, including that first podium. At the test event, they were in China, and it was just really cool to see all the pieces coming together for them. Then to be able to be a part of that, behind the scenes, doing the calls for NBC, it was a really special thing to be a part of.

"We've all been teammates for so many years. And it's hard not to get emotional on the air when these guys were making the gold happen. It was a really special thing to be a part of. Having known these guys as long as I have, and we know all the ups and downs, what we go through with life on the road and injuries and the back and forth to competitive lifestyles. And it was just a really special thing to be a part of."

Seth and I had a friendship that dated back to the start of my career. Even when we were competing against each other, Seth was somebody who would tell me stories and just be there for me. He was inducted into the Hall of Fame in 2020. He won four X Games medals, four world championship medals, and a pair of Olympic gold medals.

We had grown close after all the years of traveling together.

"We're really like a family traveling together on the road all these years," he said. "I was so proud of Nick, especially with the heartbreak from the men's event, and then turn it around, and just in getting up for the moment and being ready to do battle with all those guys that he had to race. So it was really special to get to witness that."

Koski brought up something amazing, something I couldn't even imagine. There was a time when Ishpeming was full of Olympians, because that was where they all trained. If you sat in the middle of town, there was a good chance that you would see an Olympian walk by on any given day.

"What Nick's been able to do, it really brings us back to the 1950s here in the U.P.," Koski said. "In 1950, if you're sitting right here, like 95 percent of our Olympians lived and trained right around this area. Most of them were ski jumpers, Nordic sport–type athletes. This community was reminded by Nick's accomplishments of just how many badass skiers and snowboarders come from these obscure areas."

I smiled, kind of blown away.

"We're super proud of Nick and his ties to the U.P. and going out and showing people what's happened," Koski said. "I guarantee there's gonna be more kids that grab their boards, and knock the dust off and get on the chairlift on opening day in the fall. Because if he won a gold medal, I might be able to do it. That's what they're thinking. So, we're pumped man. And Nick deserves all the credit in the world. He's a workhorse to see him go by at 6:30 in the morning in his truck, the only guy on the road heading to the gym, here in Marquette, just after winning his Olympic medal. He's been doing it for four months. So, we're excited and super proud."

That was why I wanted to give so many speeches to kids across the Upper Peninsula. I wanted to inspire them, just like Seth had.

"I know Nick is definitely in that driver's seat right now as the gold medalist of having that effect on people in the sport all across the country," Seth said. "I mean, for me, the older I get, the more that I can see how that impact affected kids and got kids inspired to do the event. It's just awesome. And so, you know, with Nick's and Lindsey's success this year, it creates a whole other wave of kids that are going to come into that program and be future Olympians, following all of our footsteps on a snowboard."

Then, I took a moment to share something that I had been wanting to say. I thanked Seth for all the kind words he said on the broadcast.

"I can't even find the words to express how special those few days were calling Lindsey's race," Seth said. "Calling your first race and then calling the team race, and you know just how proud I am of you. For me, as a new parent now, just kind of stepping into my fifth year of fatherhood, having such a different understanding of a journey you've been on all these years, it was really an incredible thing to be a part of, and I was just so proud of you."

"Yeah, well, I appreciate it," I said.

"Once you get that gold, it is so life-changing," Seth said. "You start to just have this whole different slate of experiences that you'd never had before in your career. And it allows you to reflect and have all these moments, especially with young kids, where you start to kind of really realize what that platform of being an Olympic gold medalist allows you to do. For me, I realized pretty early on, after '06, that ability to give back and inspire is what's going to have the biggest change on our sport in the long run over the coming decades. And I already see in Nick just that joy of sharing the experience."

That was the part that was still stunning to me—how this could change others.

Eventually the discussion turned to my NBC interview. "Nick, it's such a good thing," Seth said. "I think it's so important in society for the kids to see a badass, world-class athlete that has the ability to be vulnerable, because it's everything that we go through in our own journeys, and the ups and downs. Lots of times, people never see a strong guy share that kind of vulnerability. It's important for kids to see that. I really believe that."

CHAPTER 17

ONE LAST GOAL

"WHAT'S THE PLAN?" Steve Polich, who ran Ski Brule, asked me.

"What do you mean?" I asked.

We were having a meeting to set up a fundraiser at Ski Brule.

"You have to capitalize on this gold medal," Steve Polich, who owned Ski Brule and ran a successful law practice told me. "Turn this into something."

I had always shied away from that. I hated having fundraisers, and I hated asking for help. I felt like there were so many better things for people to donate to, rather than helping some 40-year-old athlete. But in reality, without help, I would never have become a pro snowboarder and I would never have had the chance to represent Team USA.

"You've got to strike quick," he said. "From a commercial standpoint, we have to know the plan."

Polich skied in college and professionally and got his master's degree and a law degree. He had a tremendous mind for business, but I just didn't have that in me. Olympians had always had a short window to cash in on their celebrity and popularity, but I just didn't care about money. If you love something, the money will take care of itself.

"That's not what life is about," I told him. "That's not what I'm doing."

Then, I told him about the schools I had visited, giving speeches. And I had several more on the schedule.

"I'll deal with money later," I said. "First, I have some schools to visit." To me, talking to kids was more important. Trying to inspire them while it was still fresh. I had an unique chance to get people to listen to me.

"What are your plans for the future?" he asked, point blank.

"I'm not done," I said.

Polich would have been surprised if I had said anything else.

"I'm going to go for it again," I said.

What did that mean? I had no idea. I figured that I would do the same thing that I had done in 2022—bust my butt, live in my van in the summer. I didn't want to live with the regret: Could I have gotten a world championship right after that gold medal? Would I make it? I wasn't sure. But I might as well try.

Chasing a world championship at 41 might sound even more crazy than anything I had ever done. But it was the only thing I knew.

I did the math. I will be 44 for the next Olympics.

But I will say this—the next Olympics is in Italy. My mom's 100 percent Italian, and all her brothers and sisters want to go.

By getting two podiums in the individual event in 2022, I knew that I would be funded for the next two seasons. That was all I needed to know. Because of that, I decided to make a run at the 2026 games. My body will let me know when I need to stop. I've always said that as long as I am competitive and having fun, which go hand in hand, I will continue to do it.

Also, perhaps as importantly, as long as the team is paying for me to fly all over the world. I will keep doing it.

For me, life is about living with as little regret as possible.

I wonder: If I put in the work, could I become a world champion at 41 years old?

So I committed to chasing that dream. And I figured, don't mess with something that works. So, I was going to do the same thing that I did last year. I was going to work out at AdvantEdge. I was going to live in my van. I was going to make the same sacrifices.

After spending a little downtime with my son.

CHAPTER 18

THE MOST IMPORTANT SPEECH OF MY LIFE

SITTING ON THE COUCH IN MY HOUSE in Iron River, I was working on a computer, tweaking the most important speech of my life. At least, it was the speech that meant the most to me.

"Are you going to wear the gold medal?" Landon, my 18-year-old son, asked.

The gold medal was on a shelf under a big-screen TV, next to a football helmet. I made that shelf out of a chunk of limestone that Jason Buechel, my good friend from Fond du Lac Natural Stone, gave me, and my buddy cut the cedar logs with his Ponsse machine to hold it up.

Turned out great, if I say so myself.

"It's not my day," I told Landon. "It's your day."

Landon was graduating from high school, and his classmates asked me to give the commencement address, which was seriously cool and a tremendous honor. I was excited and anxious, wanting to strike the right balance of anecdotes and advice, hoping to tell these kids some of the lessons I had learned on this crazy journey.

They had asked me during their homecoming parade, right before I flew off to Switzerland for a training camp before the season started. I spent the next couple months working on the speech and finding quotes I wanted to use. Then I won the Olympics and had to change the speech.

I kept going through the speech, reading it over, adding some jokes. I've always lived by a few simple rules about public speaking: keep it honest, try to make them cry, and make them laugh. If you do that, it will be a good speech.

The next day, I went to my parents' house, just a few minutes away.

"What should I wear?" I asked my mother.

"A suit," she said. "Everybody has seen you in your Olympic stuff. Nobody has ever seen you dressed up."

I was 40 years old but had never owned a suit. I never needed one—not until I won the gold. I was suddenly getting invited to different types of events. I was far more comfortable in sweats, a T-shirt, and a baseball hat. I had acquired so much Team USA clothing over the years that I hardly went anywhere without wearing some piece of Olympic gear. Besides, I was dang proud to wear the Red, White, and Blue. Dang proud of what those colors and gear represented. Not just as an athlete—I had a deep appreciation for the men and women who gave their lives and fought for me to be able to live the life I do.

"As a guest speaker, you should be dressed up," she said. "You also need a haircut."

"Yeah," I said. "I mean, I shaved the back of my neck myself. And it was less than perfect."

I laughed.

"I can see," she said, laughing.

My mom had cut my hair my entire life. She had to learn because our family was too big to be able to afford someone else doing it. She cut all our hair, all our friends' hair, and all my parents friends' hair.

"I messed up a little," I smiled.

If there was one thing people could say about me and my family, we never took ourselves too seriously.

I spent the whole first half of the day practicing my speech. This was the most important speech of my life, and I needed to know that I was ready and that I had it down. Even though I was reading off an iPad with my speech on a teleprompter in front of me, I needed to know the speech almost by heart, so I wouldn't lose my place, and so I could look up at the graduates when it was needed. No way I was leaving this to chance.

Preparation—the key to life.

———————

The graduation was held on the West Iron County High School football field—the same one where I once played, and my brothers played, and my father played.

A wooden lectern was set up on the football field, facing 39 aluminum chairs—Landon's entire graduating class. The chairs were spread out several yards apart, stretching across the middle of the field, making the class look a little bigger.

A table was set up on the track that circled the field—on the same track and in the same stadium where I had spent countless hours practicing the hurdles.

I sat on a folding chair, just like the day I graduated from high school. Only this time, I was facing the graduates. And I had a gold medal in my pocket. It felt like my life had come full-circle *after* I had taken a crazy lap around the world and ended up back home, with the most amazing thing in my pocket.

The crowd sat behind me in the metal bleachers, facing the field. Some of the parents were dressed up, wearing dress shirts and ties. But most people in the crowd were wearing blue jeans—Iron River was always a blue jeans kind of city.

"Pomp and Circumstance" played over the loudspeakers, and everybody stood up. Landon's graduating class had lined up on the other side of the football field and the kids started marching along the track, toward their seats.

The girls wore bright white gowns and sat in chairs on the left side of the field. The guys wore blue gowns and sat on the other side.

I glanced at Landon. In the program, my son was listed as Landon Sundelius.

His mother, Tina Sundelius, wanted him to have her last name. Tina and I weren't married, and she already had a son. Her first son had her last name. Even though I was there, even though I was at the hospital, she chose to give Landon her last name. She made an argument that she didn't want multiple kids under the same roof with different names. So, I could see that. For me, as a dad, I'm not going to manipulate my child and try to get him to change his name. I used other tactics. I was going to try to be as cool as I could, and be the raddest dad possible, so that when he got older, he would want to take my name. It was kind of funny; in 2010, when articles came out calling him Landon Baumgartner, I remember her being mad.

But she was fine with it now.

And I totally respected that.

———————

Shadows stretched across the field as the first few speakers talked.

Teagan Leonarduzzi, one of Landon's classmates, went to the microphone and introduced me.

"Today's guest speaker is the epitome of the phrase 'hard work pays off,'" she said. "While traveling the world training, raising his son, and working in his free time, Nick Baumgartner managed to come home and make his hometown even more proud than when he left every single time."

I was smiling hard. This was such a thrill. She listed off the highlights of my career, from my days in high school to the Olympics.

"Although Nick is proud of what he has done, he wouldn't consider any of those acts his biggest achievements," she said. "Every time anyone asks, Nick will always say his greatest accomplishment in life is his son, Landon."

I nodded my head, the emotion starting to bubble inside me.

"Baumgartner's warm heart and compassion and life are really what earned him the spot to be here today," she said. "His determination and perseverance are truly a characteristic of the Baumgartner way. With that being said, the road in front of the high school will be renamed Nick Baumgartner Way."

Wow. What a thrill.

I was presented with a green road sign with white letters that read: NICK BAUMGARTNER WAY. And tears came to my eyes. To have the road in front of the high school renamed? Wow. Just amazing.

"That is crazy—thank you guys," I said.

I stood up and grabbed the road sign, posing for a picture, the emotion stirring inside me. It was an amazing honor. Mind-blowing, really.

But I didn't want to speak about it too much, because this was their day. Not mine.

"Hey, I got an idea," I said, leaning into the microphone. "Get him up here and get him crying before he starts to speak."

Everybody laughed.

The air was cool, the sun bright. A couple hundred people sat in the bleachers, facing the field. I knew just about everybody in the crowd. I had competed in front of thousands of people in person and millions on TV. But the people in those stands meant more to me than anything.

And this moment was incredible.

"Thank you, Teagan," I said.

I took a deep breath.

"OK—thank you to everyone for everything throughout my career, which happens to be their entire lives," I started. "I've been a professional snowboarder for the past 17 years, and the support and kindness that you've all shown me and my family has been amazing. All I can say is, it's been an honor to represent you all."

My voice cracked.

Just think about all the people who have helped me.

All the businesses who sponsored me.

All the people who came out to the parade.

All the people who supported me.

Just amazing.

"To all the graduates, thank you—thank you for always making me feel like part of the group," I said. "I mean, it's not every day a parent is asked by their child and their friends to not only give them advice, but to deliver a speech on their graduation day, a day that represents the biggest accomplishments in your life to date. Heck, you even invited me on your senior class trip. So, thank you."

I was a chaperone on their trip to the Wisconsin Dells, a tourist attraction. I mean, they asked me to be a chaperone? A derelict like me? It just cracked me up.

But it also made me tremendously proud to be in their lives.

I just hoped that I was making a big impact on them.

"Let me just say how incredibly proud I am of every single one of you," I said. "It's been such a pleasure to watch you all grow up. Although I'm not really sure how you guys grew up and matured, and I never did. But that's for another day."

Thankfully, everybody laughed. Maybe this was gonna work after all.

"It's been such a pleasure to watch you all navigate life and overcome the struggles to get here today," I said. "Some of you had to work a lot harder than others. Maybe school didn't come as easy for you. Maybe you had too many distractions, too much on your plate, too much going on at home. Regardless, you have all overcome many distractions and many obstacles."

Everybody has obstacles. Everybody has challenges. Everybody has to overcome...something. Whether it was the kids on that field or the parents in the stands, I just want my story to inspire them. I want them to feel like everything is possible. I want them to look at the medal and realize anything is possible.

"You've all lived through the invention of the smartphone and tablets," I told the graduates. "You survived putting in an insane amount of screen time playing Minecraft and Fortnite and sending pictures of the ceiling or up your nostrils just to keep a streak alive."

Everybody laughed.

"You survived participation medals," I said.

OK, so that was a dig. I hate the idea of participation medals. If there was one thing I knew, there was always a winner and a loser. That's life. That's the story that has defined my life. Participation trophies make people soft. Losing teaches far more important lessons.

"Last but definitely not least, you made it through a global pandemic," I said. "Rather than learning about history, you lived through a history lesson. I really hope that you understand how amazing this accomplishment is. I hope you take some confidence from this and move on knowing that you can accomplish any-thing you want. You are all Yoopers—tough and adaptable. You have that grit and tenacity to help you get through any obstacle in your way."

I took a breath.

"Here are a couple things that I have learned while learning this parenting thing," I said. "Kids don't always listen to their parents. And they seldom ask or seek our opinion. Being the awesome parents that we are, it never stopped us from giving it and annoying you every single day."

My own parents sat in the stands. They had always been there for me, always been there for Landon. I couldn't thank them enough.

"Now I just hope that I can make you all proud, proud and happy to ask me to speak today," I said. "But if I lay an egg up here, if it doesn't go well, just remember, you made this decision. And as you move forward in life, your decisions have bigger con-sequences."

That point was so important for me. It wasn't a throwaway line. Life is about making decisions; it's about the choices you make along the way. Every decision will bring a consequence, good or bad. And you have to live with them. You have to learn from them.

"Before I start giving you advice to help you along your jour-ney of life, or cram my opinion into your brains, I want to assure you all that what I say today is in no way a message from your teachers, or something relayed from your parents," I said. "Well, except for you, Landon. That's exactly what this is. You all had your chances. Now it's my turn."

I glanced at Principal Mike Berutti, who had been my football coach. And the proud parent of one of the graduates.

"Don't worry, Coach, you don't have to cut the mic," I said. "But I do want you all to know that if you don't like the advice that I give today, at least you can take comfort in the fact that you don't have to wonder if this is the same advice that I would give to my own child."

I took a deep breath.

"I thought long and hard about the most important things I have learned in this crazy attempt at life that I could pass on to you as you start the next chapter of yours," I said. "Since I sat right where you're sitting today, I know that every graduate here has the knowledge and the talent to succeed. But what I want to know is: Do you have the guts to fail? The biggest thing I want you all to know is that failure is part of the process. If you're not failing, you're not even trying. When it happens, make sure you learn from it. And then keep moving forward. Your entire lives. I have pushed 'Dream Big' on you. Anytime I signed a poster or your shirt, I tagged it with 'Dream Big.' You guys have an amazing opportunity to go out and do anything that you want. I urge you not to sell yourself short. I urge you to 'Dream Big.' Go out there and take some risks and chase what you love. If you don't know what that is yet, that's okay. Start trying things. Since failure is part of the process, don't let your fear of failure stop you from finding what it is you are truly meant to do. Here's a fun question to ask yourself: What would you attempt to do if you knew you couldn't fail? Think about that."

I started telling stories from my career.

Overcoming injuries.

Overcoming failures.

Overcoming adversity.

Most of them knew the stories. They had lived all of those moments with me. They had lived them with Landon.

"I want to share one more story with you guys," I said. "And this story is one that everyone knows. After falling short and failing at three different Olympics spanning more than 12 years, I decided to attempt to qualify for a fourth and try to achieve the goal that I had made 17 years prior. Knowing this could be my last, I worked harder than I ever had in the past. Not only did I make sacrifices, but my son had to make a bunch as well. And I'm so grateful for that. He had to have me absent while I isolated for COVID. He had to let me go for weeks and months at a time to chase this dream. We had to live quite frugally at times because I chose to chase this dream for passion, not for money. And I hope you guys do as well.

"I wanted to show you all what is possible if you push yourself and try to achieve greatness. And I hope that with this journey and my actions, I've showed you that in order to achieve great things, you must make sacrifices. For you, it might look like skipping parties to get your work done. Getting sleep and not wilding out every night, spending weekends not escaping the life you have—but building the life you want. If you make those sacrifices, I promise, you will get to have fun for way longer in life. If you go too hard right away, you will make life very hard on yourself. So be willing to make those sacrifices because it's so worth it.

"This past offseason, I knew a lot of people doubted me. I had people ask me if I really thought I could make the U.S. Olympic Snowboard Team at 40. I heard people say that I needed to grow up and let this dream go. To everyone that doubted me, I thank you. Because it was a big motivation for me. I love when someone tells me I can't do something. Tell me I can't, and I will prove to the world that I can. Because I'm a Yooper, and I'm a Wykon."

My voice cracked with emotion.

"I've had to fight so hard to get to where I am," I said. "And even harder to stay here. I've had to make my own opportunities, because no one was going to hand me anything. But fighting for this, and pushing and working harder than anyone else, by not believing the excuses that we are from too small of a town, too small of a school—and for me, too small of a mountain—I set myself up for success. And I did this all while failing over and over along the way."

I finished by talking about the 2022 Olympics. About finishing my race and looking up the mountain at Lindsey. Putting all my hope in my partner.

"Once I finished, I immediately started to cheer and scream for my partner," I said. "We've been teammates for 17 years. And we have encouraged, motivated, and pushed each other to unbelievable heights. You guys, it's so important to surround yourself with this caliber of people. They say you become the average of the five people you hang out with the most. So be very careful what type of people you let into your circle moving forward. And more than anything, I want you guys to know that when Lindsey crossed that finish line, and we won, and I got to realize a dream that I had worked half my life for…"

My voice was quavering.

"And I knew I was going to be able to bring it home," I said. "That feeling is a feeling I hope each and every one of you get to experience in your life. 'Cause I know you are all capable."

I stood with my hands in my pockets, the emotion bursting inside me.

"So I ask you again: What would you attempt to do if you knew you couldn't fail?"

I paused. To me, that was the key to everything. Unbridled passion. With no fear.

"I hope you can remember these lessons that I've learned along my long career," I said. "You will never succeed more than you fail. Just know, every time you fail, you are one step closer to success. So don't let it cripple you. Learn from it. Keep your head up and keep moving forward. Don't ever lose that inner dreamer who wants to go conquer the world. Keep dreaming big. Also remember that dreams should be massive. If your dreams don't scare you, they aren't big enough. So go out there and be scared. Be terrified. But be relentless in your efforts to get what you want out of life. Also remember that dreams alone are just that. They are just dreams, so you have to work hard. You have to set goals. And here is an interesting fact about setting goals. Just by writing a goal down, you are 40 percent more likely to achieve it. I promise you, nothing in life comes that easy. So I would take a free 40 percent and I would write down your goals. It's also important that you make sacrifices to set yourself up for success. Find what you love and try to do that at all costs. Don't chase money. Chase happiness. Live your life, not someone else's. Put in the work and be prepared for opportunity. Because if you cut corners and fall short, I promise you will regret it.

"And finally, I've been able to compete at four Olympics because I overcame adversity. I failed and didn't let it stop me. I didn't listen to the people who told me that I couldn't, and I didn't worry about the past. I learned from it and kept moving forward. Thank you guys for having me. I hope my story inspires you to go get exactly what you want out of life. And now, once again, what would you attempt to do if you knew you couldn't fail? Answer that question and go do that. Thank you, guys."

Somebody screamed and everybody started applauding.

I ended the speech and took my seat. A few minutes later, Landon walked across the stage with his diploma, and I sprang out of my chair. I kneeled, pulled out my cell phone, and started videotaping him. Tears were in my eyes.

I was wearing my Olympic ring, still covered with concrete. The gold medal was in my pocket.

But the Olympics were the furthest thing from my mind. I looked at Landon, at my amazing son, who had grown up and was starting his own journey. Starting his own path.

And I've never been so proud in my life.